The IPM Guide to
COST-EFFECTIVE
RECRUITMENT
John Courtis

GW00630916

Institute of Personnel Management

John Courtis qualified as a Chartered Accountant, was commissioned in the RAF and then spent five years with Ford Motor Co before moving to consultancy in Reed Executive, EAL and finally, John Courtis and Partners. He has added to his industrial experience in recent years as a non-executive director and Chairman of Deeko plc. He is also a Vice-Chairman of the Federation of Recruitment and Employment Services.

This mix has given the author managerial experience in large and small organizations and staff recruitment experience as consultant and employer. He has to live with the results of his own recruitment which is rare amongst search and selection consultants. He is also active in management education.

Previous books include the first edition of this guide, under the same title, *Money Matters For Management, Out of Work, Communicating For Results, Annual Reports as an Aid to Profit, Less Data – More Profit, Decimate Your Overheads* and *The Candidate's Guide to the Management Job Hunt.*

Phototypeset by Tameside Filmsetting Ltd, Ashton-under-Lyne, Lancashire
Printed in Great Britain by R. J. Acford, Chichester

British Library Cataloguing Publication Data

Courtis, John
The IPM Guide to Cost-Effective Recruitment
Second edition
1. Recruiting of employees
1. Title   2. Institute of Personnel Management
658.3, 11   HS 5549.5R44
ISBN 0 85292 340 6

Foreword

In any organization, whether in the public or the private sector, results can only be achieved through people. Indeed, the only way one company can outstrip its rivals is by attracting and retaining a more effective team of employees, managers and directors. People constitute the principal asset of an organization; consequently one of the prime tasks confronting management is to maintain and, if possible, to improve this crucial asset. Peter Drucker has emphasized that: 'Management's main objective should be to select the managers of tomorrow'. Fiercer competition, both nationally and internationally, is not the only reason why efficient selection has become an increasingly important issue. Legislation during recent years has made it more difficult and more expensive to remove incompetent, unsatisfactory, or inappropriate staff today. A reduction in the number of selection mistakes can improve the balance sheet.

Despite the obvious importance of systematic selection, recruitment procedures in Britain tend to be haphazard. Paradoxically the more senior the appointment, the greater is the probability of a superficial and inadequate approach. Directors join the boards of major British companies by methods which are mysterious in the extreme. Job descriptions and person specifications are rare commodities in the boardroom and great is the probability that the Personnel Department will not have been involved in the process. If there is any expertise in selection (and I believe that there is) it is reasonable to anticipate that expertise will reside within the personnel function.

There is no golden rule about the best method of selection. Press advertisements, headhunting, personal contacts and staff recommendations all have their place. The fundamental test is: does the procedure provide the correct result? All selection, by whatever method, is an act of prediction. The success, or failure, of a selection process cannot be measured until the performance of the person appointed is appraised. Nevertheless the reliability and validity of selection decisions by personnel managers and line managers can be improved significantly by a systematic and thorough approach. John Courtis provides a sound practical guide for anyone determined to reduce the incidence of selection mistakes. Furthermore, for the cost-conscious, his advice could lead to financial economies and/or better value in terms of personnel budget expenditure.

Historically, Britain has tended to neglect recruitment and selection systems and devote a disproportionate amount of money, time and energy to training. As a consequence, many training programmes are attempts to redress selection errors. If the advice of John Courtis is followed and 'the right people are placed in the right place at the right time', subsequent training efforts can become expansive rather than corrective.

Richard S Stokes
6 December 1984

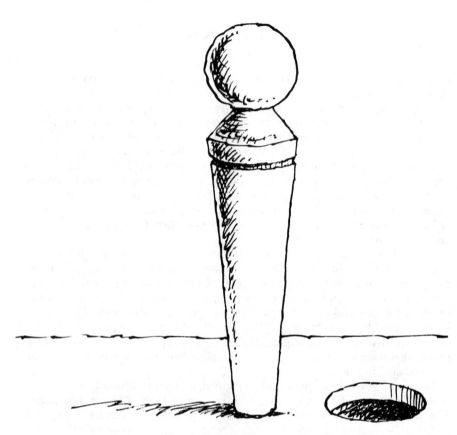

We put more of these into these than any other newspaper.

Every weekday the Daily Telegraph makes life easier for personnel managers with vacancies to fill.

It delivers more ABC1 readers than all the other quality dailies put together. And because it carries more recruitment advertising than any other national newspaper, qualified applicants look first at the Daily Telegraph.

For rates and other details please contact Paul Scott on 01-583 3939.

Daily Telegraph

Contents

72,092
qualified accountants in the UK each week

AccountancyAge

the highest circulation to

the highest readership by

the largest jobs marketplace for

qualified accountants of any UK publication

A first class response needs a first class medium

Hi-tech recruitment starts here

It's something we know all about. Because our journals are big in the world of high technology. Many are market leaders, including Electronics Weekly, Computer Weekly and Electrical Review. So if you're looking for top quality computer personnel, electronics engineers or electrical engineers, use the journals they use. It's the most cost-effective way to reach specialist technical personnel.

Just telephone Brian Durrant, Group Advertisement Manager, on 01-661 3106

ELECTRICAL-ELECTRONIC PRESS
QUADRANT HOUSE, THE QUADRANT, SUTTON, SURREY SM2 5AS

1

The objective

To avoid confusion, it is important to recognize that recruiting and employing people are not in themselves acceptable objectives. Employers have an obligation to provide equality of opportunity in employment, but they are not normally there to provide employment as such. The objective for most organizations is profit or a cost-effective service. It follows that 'vacancies' may not be an automatic prelude to recruitment. The employers' obligations to shareholders or to the community may make headcount reduction a better route to profitability or efficiency.

This context must affect attitudes to recruitment. It has to be cost-effective on two levels. First, the recruitment process itself must achieve a reasonable balance between cost and results. Second, the employment which follows must be worthwhile to both employer and employee. This does *not* mean that financial justification is the only criterion. Saving money, regardless of the side effects, is seldom justified in business. A proper balance between the cost and the quality of results is the aim.

In recruitment this is particularly important because there is an additional matter to be considered, ie the balance between speed and expense. Cost, quality and time interact. The timing pressures also impinge on the normal running of the organization. The priorities of a well run recruitment exercise can conflict with the operational priorities of the organization. It is essential that those involved recognize that recruitment ought to have a high priority, for two reasons:

(a) Recruitment yields new employees whose presence, after the induction period, will ease pressure on existing employees.

(b) Losing a day in recruitment can cost a week or more in the media and thus in the programme as a whole. Losing a week in the interviewing process can cost a month in a successful candidate's period of notice. At worst, it can lose the best candidate, too.

2

Alternatives to recruitment

Too many organizations recruit without considering the full range of alternatives. Some do not recognize any. 'Vacancies', whether new or replacements, may be opportunities to save on salaries, prove that the management development system works or retrieve someone who is leaving another job. The most important point is that the alternatives should be considered early in the process, not at the end, from expediency.

Doing the right thing promptly and well looks good. Doing it three months late, after everyone involved has been demotivated, looks shabby and may even be the catalyst which makes other people consider leaving. To identify the right thing, ask:

(a)   Could we get by without the job being done at all?
(b)   Could its component parts be allocated to other staff?
(c)   Do the benefits derived from the job justify the total cost of filling it, year in, year out?
(d)   If we had to have a 10 per cent headcount reduction programme, would we eliminate this job (not quite the same question as in (a) and it is important that it be asked separately)?
(e)   If the answers to the above questions do not eliminate the job, can you:

      (i)   mechanize it?
      (ii)   subcontract it?

If the answer is 'no' to both of these there are still several credible and respectable alternatives before recruitment is inevitable. These include:

(a)   Internal promotion or sideways development moves.
(b)   Offering the job to someone who is serving his or her notice (even in small organizations it is easy to forget a redundant employee who is out of sight).

(c) Reviewing future workloads to see if the job is an all the year round
     one and whether it will be the same in 12 or 18 months. Is it, for
     instance, affected by current or planned computerization? Does it
     exist to supervise people who may shortly not need supervision? Is it
     supporting a moribund product line? Is it supporting a growth
     situation which may stabilize and need less attention?

All these situations could dictate the use of temporary staff, part-timers,
people just back from overseas who would welcome a temporary role (even
though they would not do the job on a long-term basis) and finally staff who
are hanging on grimly until they can reach retirement age or the earliest
point at which they can take early retirement. Any one of these can turn a
vacancy into an opportunity.

The calculated risk

If we consider some of the above alternatives in relation to specific cases,
there may still be opposition to using internal candidates. Sometimes this is
right and there may be merit in buying fresh talent, skills or experience into
a key function. A good development plan will have identified the ways an
organization should be training and coaching people and even if the
vacancy occurs earlier than plans forecast, employees nowadays are
accustomed to quicker personal development than their predecessors.
Taking a risk on someone earlier than you or the victim/beneficiary
anticipated is usually good for morale.

The classic error is to compare the internal candidates, whose weak
points are known, against external candidates who are trying fairly hard to
suppress their weaknesses and highlight their virtues. In these
circumstances, unless selection techniques are flawless, the external
candidate who looks 90 per cent right should be rejected in favour of the
internal runner-up who scores 80 per cent, not least because recruiters
forget to adjust for time, money and effort spent in the learning period.

There are other factors which favour the internal risk. Given that you
know his or her defects you can train to eliminate them or structure the job
to compensate for them. Furthermore, the job gets filled quickly and there
is better continuity. Also, you may have the chance to promote someone
who is an unexciting subordinate because his job is undemanding, into a
managerial job which actually suits his or her talents better. This is
particularly true in companies where some functions demand high
intellectual levels. The graduate whose analytical competence is the

3

measure of achievement in a junior post may have no chance to demonstrate the rarer managerial talents which are needed in a more senior post.

Reallocating tasks among the peer group is also possible. If combined with a positive attempt to delegate tasks and objectives from that group to the line below them on the organization chart, the vanished vacancy can give a boost to several people whom conventional promotions would not have touched for months or years. This exercise can sometimes be combined with wider mechanization, which nowadays includes the introduction or expansion of computer use.

Moving people sideways can be misunderstood, unless it is a declared part of your management development policy. Some companies avoid taking back people who are in the process of leaving, whether they are redundant, voluntary departures, early retirers or other special cases. These cases vary, so that the possibility of keeping the leaver should be considered in the company's interests without worrying too much whether the company will look 'silly'. Similarly, when considering subcontracting, perhaps to one of those departing employees or to a totally independent operation, the company's current best interests are more important than past doctrine, unless significant industrial relations problems would result. The same applies to a move to part-time staffing, the use of temporaries (cost-effective and flexible if well used), or recruiting on a job-sharing basis.

It cannot be stressed too strongly how important it is that those involved address their minds to the alternatives before starting external recruitment. Delay or omission costs money, time and goodwill. Careful thought about the alternatives also puts later external recruitment in the right context in two ways. First, if there is genuinely no internal solution, everyone is dedicated to spending money and time properly to get an external candidate under offer promptly. Secondly, if the decision to go outside is marginal, it can be reversed quickly and confidently when the open market turns out to be less productive than expected.

Other reasons for doing thorough research at this stage include the sophistication of computer technology. Tasks that could not have been delegated to a novice and a computer two years ago may be considered today, for three reasons: computers are cheaper; the software and hardware is continually improving; employees in general are more familiar with computers.

4

3

Job descriptions

This chapter examines the use of narrative job descriptions and specifications as an aid to recruitment. It is not an exhaustive text on job analysis or the best way to research and produce a job description. For such guidance see *How to write a job description* by Bernard Ungerson and *Job evaluation; objectives and methods* by George Thomason.

The internal document is usually produced in a structured, formalized style which is ideal for internal use but inappropriate as a positive tool in recruitment. There is a powerful case for rewriting the core content in an easily assimilated narrative which also offers data on the company, the candidate requirement and the rewards and conditions. But first, consider the reasons for having the document. It must help recruiters to gather their thoughts. It must aid communication with future employees. It must assist communication within the organization and avoid misunderstandings about the objectives for the job-holder. Putting a signature to a document does not guarantee comprehension, so it is preferable to ask people above and around the job to record their own views of objectives and job content before the text is finalized. This is an essential part of the process of job analysis. The discipline of putting things on paper is vital. For example, gathering together in one place a clear statement of job content, the ideal and minimum candidate requirements, rewards and place in the structure gives the first chance to consider whether the recruitment process is viable without one or more of these being changed. This is true whether looking for unskilled labour or for general management.

The document will be read by one or more candidates at some stage, so it is important that it is not boring, turgid, task-oriented or riddled with jargon. Ideally it should be a marketing document for the company and the job.

Early action

The first step in assembling a new job description is to find the previous one. Even if it is alleged that none exists, keep on asking. Although sometimes nobody will admit to having seen one, repeated enquiry will disclose its existence. Secretaries are rather better than managers at finding them. At the same time, ask the present incumbent to write one, preferably without reference to the historic document. Also ask the person to whom the job holder reports to outline what he or she wants out of the job and/or the department it heads.

Editing

Unless your colleagues are exceptional two things will happen. First, there will be substantial differences between what was specified last time, what the jobholder thinks it is now and what the manager actually wants from it. Secondly, there will be many tasks and no objectives.

The objectives are vital. Without them you cannot decide whether the job should exist at all. Seek them assiduously. If you can find none, there is a considerable chance that the job is irrelevant and therefore redundant. It follows that the job description needs to be assembled before you decide whether to recruit or to avoid recruitment.

The importance of the objectives in relation to corporate and local objectives will also help to make other decisions about the qualitative requirements in the candidate specification and the urgency of the search. This also affects the allocation of resources to the task.

Minimum content

The finished document should contain the following data at the very least:

(a) the job title (and a translation if your organization uses obscure, dated, generalized or status-conscious titles)
(b) to whom job reports
(c) the essential objective(s)
(d) the extent of personal responsibility for the achievement of those objectives
(e) key tasks
(f) key contacts in and outside the organization
(g) authority over assets, spending and people

(h) working conditions, ie place, times, special environment
(i) problems and constraints

Repeatedly, when advising on lower level staff appointments or when being involved in shop-floor hiring, the author has been told politely or otherwise that the minimum specified above is excessive. The usual argument is that the candidates don't need it or won't understand much of it. This is unacceptable. If it cannot be understood, the document needs to be made more intelligible. Any employee must benefit from a clearer understanding of why he or she is needed. The point about objectives is a good example. If the employee only knows the tasks without knowing the reason for the tasks, he or she may assume an objective different from or wholly opposed to the real one and use initiative in the wrong direction. It is no use saying that Fred or Noreen have no initiative. Everyone has some. The key to controlling them is to make sure they have enough information to use it in the right direction or at least not to apply it in the wrong direction.

Peripheral data

An organization chart can be useful at management and supervisory levels, together with a brief description of the company's activities or the local contribution to them. Even if one is not issuing the text to candidates, there may be other sites in the same group where employees are unclear about local activities.

Similarly, an explicit statement of the range in which an initial salary offer can be made is important. If the document will be seen by candidates, a clear statement of benefits must be added. It is essential that employers do not fudge the issue of wages/salaries by keeping a bit in reserve 'for the ideal candidate'. If they do not declare the limit, they will not attract the ideal, except by accident and recruitment is not about accidents or luck.

Candidate specification

Finally, the candidate requirement. This must include the minimum need. Specifying the ideal and being forced to compromise later is not always successful. By all means have an ideal. State it at the outset and then consider why it would be better to have someone near the ideal rather than at the minimum level. Those involved will learn more about the job and aid the planning of the recruitment programme, but if anyone is tempted to avoid defining the minimum, there are major hazards in store. For instance:

9

(a)   Spending considerable time and money looking for the unattainable ideal and then having to start again to get the minimum

(b)   the salary is out of line with the ideal specified so nobody replies and one has to repeat the exercise at a higher salary

(c)   the ideal is so far away from the minimum that the ideal candidate perceives the job as beneath him or her regardless of salary

(d)   when employers later compromise away from the ideal, they select someone *below* the minimum need because nobody has defined the minimum clearly or at all.

(e)   in the absence of a clear baseline, everyone regards the previous job holder as the minimum, forgetting that he or she was much less experienced when hired.

The list could be much longer. If the ideal gets translated into the advertisement as a minimum requirement and there are no ideal people around willing to consider that job at that price, you have managed to frighten off all the less than ideal people who would have replied if you had been more flexible, many of whom could do the job quite well.

Quality control

This brings us to a quality versus time problem. There are some jobs which have to be done well or not at all. At the other extreme, some jobs need to be done soon, but not to a high degree of precision. The manufacture of explosives is a good example of the former. Rubbish collection fits the latter.

There are also jobs in which better personal performance leads to better corporate performance. Careful analysis when specifying can help you choose between:

(a)   a basic candidate hired soon

(b)   an ideal candidate hired, of necessity, less quickly

(c)   an ideal candidate hired soon, regardless of cost

(d)   a basic candidate hired slowly.

The first two, although not always easy, are feasible given correct tactics and resources. The third is difficult but attacks the problem with a proper sense of urgency and priority. The fourth is suspect. If you can afford to be without someone in the job for an unpredictable time and when it is filled a fairly basic candidate is considered acceptable, perhaps the job could be eliminated or it has seasonal peaks which make it essentially one for temporary support.

Minimum misfits

There is a classic error in specifying the minimum candidate requirement. Employers and recruiters of all kinds display a tendency to specify qualifications which are needed only for a small part of the job and are wasted for the rest of the time. There is often an element of indirect discrimination in this.

For example, if the true requirement is for the intelligence normally associated with a graduate sample but the job does not use specific material from a particular syllabus or the thought processes and research skills believed to be honed by university experience, the minimum should actually be someone who meets university entry standards, not degree passes. Other people may demand a qualified accountant for certain legal or fiscal knowledge in the syllabus. Someone who has passed the relevant papers in the final examination (or even the intermediate) may be the right minimum level and be better value. Similarly, requiring 'O' and 'A' level passes in volume is likely to be more for the recruiters' comfort than for real needs. Guard against this. As a general rule, formal testing for the specific needs of the known job is likely to be more effective than historic academic achievements.

Inadvertent discrimination

Another possible pitfall is that the job specification may require overly specific experience which achieves discrimination against some minority groups. It is very important that the finished specification is reviewed with this possibility in mind. If possible, to follow the spirit of legislation rather than the letter, the aim should be to eliminate all unreasonable discrimination rather than just the areas currently covered by legislation. If one has colleagues suspected of unreasoning prejudices, it is important that they realize how difficult it is going to be to find someone competent. A sense of desperation is more likely to reduce discrimination than overt attacks on people's bias. In these circumstances, bigots are eventually grateful to find anyone who fits the specification well. Their motives may not be perfect but the result is correct. However, unless they are under some pressure, they may cling to the secret hope that they can get away with waiting for a suave male 'WASP' rather than the many competent alternatives they fear or dislike.

Involve reactionary people in the last stage of the candidate analysis and this will help all concerned to look at the requirement generated and work out carefully how many people within reasonable travelling distance actually fit this requirement, how few of them might be mobile this year, how many of that minority would want to work for you and whether you can reach any of them without unreasonable expense. The catchment area requirement is more real now than it has ever been. Disparities in housing costs, spouses in fulltime jobs, difficulties in moving children between schools and unwillingness to move to areas of higher unemployment all combine to reduce mobility substantially. This will also affect the sources of recruitment which will be suitable to your search.

Race, employment and the law

The level of unemployment among black people is twice as high as it is for white people.

It is not because black people lack qualifications — in many cases they have more than their white contemporaries. It's because many employers discriminate. Some deliberately, but many more because they have practices which effectively hold back black Britons.

For example, do you select people on the basis of written tests where the ability to write English is not necessary for the job? By doing so, you might be putting people whose first language is not English at a disadvantage.

Or do you recruit by "word-of-mouth"? If you do and if your workforce is mainly white, you're probably excluding most black applicants.

Parliament has approved a Code of Practice which contains practical recommendations on how to avoid this type of discrimination.

For a free copy contact the
Commission for Racial Equality, Elliot House, 10-12 Allington Street, London SW1E 5EH. Telephone 01-828 7022.

Because you need
talented professionals

contact Benton & Bowles Recruitment. The only
agency in Britain to win the Blue Riband Express
Recruitment Award three years in a row.
To give yourself a winning chance, get in touch
with Roger Taylor or John Stainer.

199 Knightsbridge, London SW7 1RP. Telephone 01-589 1444.

4

Sources of recruitment

There are considerable savings in direct costs to be made from matters covered in this chapter, but greater savings (both in direct costs and management time) will always be derived by avoiding the misdirected expenditure of money and time covered in earlier and later chapters. Even the best source will not correct major errors in the candidate specification or delay, incompetence and prejudice in the later selection process.

Equally, recruitment does not automatically imply advertising. The majority of recruitment could take place without advertising support, yet many jobs which are not advertised should be. This is not a paradox, just a simple case of inadequate planning, ignorance or prejudice. Every recruitment exercise is different from the one before. Even if the one before was for an identical job, the mere existence of the previous effort may dictate a different approach in its wake. The checklist of sources one needs to consider at this stage includes:

Advertising
Employment agencies and jobcentres/Job points/PER
Registers
Selection consultants
Search consultants (headhunters)
Outplacement consultants
Introductions by existing staff or unions
People you know already
People who have left the organization
People who applied last time
Other volunteers, ie casual callers and correspondents
Milkround/schools contacts.

Advertising

Advertising is covered in detail in chapters 5 and 6. It constitutes the most important single source, although not a majority source. Consider it seriously against the alternatives listed later in this chapter. Correctly planned, it can be effective and cost-effective.

Consider too the use of a reputable recruitment advertising agency. The best of these offer a substantial knowledge of media and copy requirements which is available virtually free as their income arises in the form of a discount from the media's normal space charges. Do not waste time with a product or service advertising agency. The expertise is substantially different.

Before considering alternative sources, the context should be clear. The context, externally, is the recruitment marketplace, which may hold very few people relevant to a specific job and even less who can either be reached or would be interested. An awareness of the level of difficulty likely to be encountered is a vital prelude to the sourcing programme. It broadens one's attitude to the less likely or even unfashionable sources. It also disciplines the recruiter to allocate adequate resources early in the programme rather than losing time through a wholly predictable lack of response to an inadequate initial effort.

Discipline is important. Good recruitment is not about happy accidents, flair and good luck. It is very much about doing things consistently, correctly and on time. Advertising is frequently blamed for poor results which are really attributable to errors on the employer's side. Some of the other sources described below suffer similarly.

Employment agencies

Employment agencies should be considered as likely sources for clerical staff and labour. They are also effective, if properly briefed, when sourcing temporary or contract staff and labour. They are less effective at more senior levels although a few specialist outfits disprove this. They are at their best with undemanding candidate specifications. If the job is going to be difficult to fill it is statistically unlikely that any one agency will have the right candidate on file and the 'success only' nature of their fees limits the amount of time they can spend on such a problem unless they have a special relationship with the employer.

Employment agencies can be very good, very bad or somewhere in between. Most are in between. The employer, by careful selection and communication, can avoid the worst and improve the rest, before deciding whether a special relationship with one or more is workable.

Selecting agencies has probably got to be on a trial and error basis. Membership of the Federation of Recruitment and Employment Services is one useful indicator and the Federation has a code of conduct which goes beyond the fairly basic requirements of the Employment Agencies Act. The agencies' response to an employer's initial approach is also a helpful guide. If the information volunteered by the employer is clear, comprehensive and precise, accompanied by an explicit mention of any flexibility in the candidate specification, this creates a very clear yardstick against which the agencies' performance can be judged. Most may be tempted to offer candidates who are slightly outside the preferred specification. This is tolerable once, but must be met with a restatement of the criteria.

At this point the agencies will divide into three categories, demonstrating:

(a) frenetic activity, reducing to a limited and relevant response when the employers' needs are understood
(b) frenetic activity, deaf to employers' pleas
(c) limited but relevant response, which may include thoughtful comment on rewards versus candidate requirement.

Both (a) and (c) types are worth cultivating and can be turned into a useful extension of personnel resources. Their ability to react to additional disclosures is a valid and continuing quality check. So is your view of their candidate assessments.

Registers

Registers are useful as an alternative to employment agencies. It is necessary to remember that they are paper factories and in general do not interview the people whose paper records they circulate. This is not a criticism. Replies to advertisements are on the same footing. Expect a worse candidate drop-out rate than with agencies.

Selection consultants

There are several good reasons for using selection consultants, as listed below, although they are necessary only in a minority of cases:

(a) When the employer's staff do not have time to do the bulk of the recruitment exercise in-house.

(b) When the need is genuinely for selection, not just the uncritical recruitment of pairs of hands.

(c) When advice is needed on the sourcing of a rare specialist in a difficult function or sector. This implies access to relevant candidate files as well as relevant knowledge.

(d) When such files can reduce or eliminate the cost of advertising.

(e) When anonymity is essential and it is felt that the confidential reply services of advertising agencies will not be trusted by sensitive candidates.

Consider using them in all these cases, but consider also that specialist agencies at one end or search consultants at the other may be relevant. Most selection consultants have a declared salary limit below which they are not prepared to recruit and an undeclared upper limit above which they do not handle much business because it goes to search firms! The lower limit makes sense for the employer too, because it recognizes what the consultants have learned about the effectiveness and cost-effectiveness of their service. The upper limit is open to debate. See the later notes on search consultants.

How should selection consultants be selected? There are several hundred in the UK. All profess competence. Many profess to be generalist. The following filters may be helpful:

(a) Identify (from Executive Grapevine) which firms nearby allege a specialization relevant to the vacancy (by function and sector).

(b) Ask this minority, by telephone, if they are interested in handling such a vacancy and whether their candidate files would permit them to achieve a shortlist without extensive advertising. The logic offered is actually more important than the answer. For example, a refusal to tackle the job except with national advertising may be the correct reaction with a very difficult job. In all cases, an unwillingness to be involved except on the right basis (correct salary, adequate advertising, viable candidate specification) is a good sign.

(c) Ask about their fees. Test their willingness to act on a contingency basis. Again, the cheapest answer is not necessarily the best. Any firm which is taking considerable contingency (success only fees) work where the success rate is low (because employers are multiple-sourcing and/or are not sure whether they want to fill the job at all) can afford to spend only a fraction of the time on each vacancy by comparison with the time allocated to a retained exclusive assignment. This reflects in the quality of the results. Excessive eagerness to work on contingency is a bad sign.

(d) Ask for a client referee, preferably one known to you.

All these tests apply equally with search consultants and, both with selection and search firms, it is politic to ask their views on sourcing. The better consultants will probably tell potential clients if their preferred techniques are inappropriate in a particular case. For example, consultants who depend largely on advertising response for their success should warn you that a search is necessary when there are only a few dozen potential candidates in the country for a highly specialist £50,000 job. (Equally, search consultants should suggest that advertising is more appropriate if asked to find a £15,000 specialist management type of whom many hundred examples exist.) Remember the ones who decline to act. They are probably prone to perform above average on those assignments they will handle.

Most selection consultants have sound files which may enable them to work small miracles on difficult vacancies. Typically, they will not sell access to the files but they know that their existence permits them to compete against agencies and headhunters with quiet confidence. The fact that you treat them as consultants rather than as agencies also helps, if not you probably will not get value for money. There are other benefits. Consultants with relevant functional or sector experience may be better able to interview candidates and sell the job and the company to them. Senior candidates may be more willing to approach them than they would be to make direct contact or to register with an agency or the PER.

There is one other bonus. Consultants working on retained assignments can devote all their time, effort and ingenuity to solving the recruitment problem and it is often recruitment sourcing rather than selection which you need to buy, even at senior levels. This includes 'search' work. Headhunters do not have a monopoly on the technique. Most selection consultants use it where appropriate unless ethically inhibited. How do you choose consultants? Again, it is difficult not to be wholly impartial, but they should have done work for enough people for you to find a client referee whose judgement you trust and they should have been in existence long enough to be credible, and also for their files to be credible.

Search consultants

Headhunting is vital in some cases. When seeking a specialist in a discrete function or sector and there are only dozens or at most a few hundred in the country, search techniques are essential. Alas, many clients have poor experiences with headhunters because they choose them at the wrong time and for the wrong reasons. The same criteria apply in choosing them as with selection consultants. Also, do your analysis of the likely candidate bank with some care.

The analysis of the candidate bank needs explanation. Search consultants rely on a number of sources for their shortlists. Some have massive historic data in a particular commercial or industrial sector. Others have the same but by function rather than sector. Most have good contacts in their preferred areas whom they can use for opinions rather than as candidates. Some are equipped to deploy their own research teams very quickly to do new research as and when a particular need arises but do not bother to update until a need arises. Finally, they attract volunteers in large quantities. All of this gives them massive data banks. A few searching questions should show which of these are likely to be applied to your particular case. Beware those firms which are too strong in a particular sector or function. They may be ethically inhibited from searching within companies you want to poach from because of an existing client relationship with them. Similarly, their massive files may tempt them to source largely from file, rather than researching for your specific need.

If the case for headhunting is not wholly clear, consider using one of the outfits which mixes search and advertising, so that you can choose to mix the two if appropriate.

Outplacement consultants

When the first edition was written, the author was fairly sceptical about the merits of outplacement consultants. His views have reversed. Not only do they do a reasonable job for their clients (who are job hunters) but they can also be a useful additional source of middle and senior management candidates, in conventional functions and occasionally for unusual ones. If you care to establish relations with the bigger ones, they will react intelligently to a clear candidate specification, particularly if you are able to disclose the full job description in confidence. Better still, as their fees come from ex-employers or the candidates themselves, the service to you can be free. Do not expect them to have scarce categories of young high-flyers in stock. Do use them when you want competent mature managers.

Staff introductions

This source is often useful but can be made more so if you formalize it and perhaps pay a nominal bonus for successful introductions. One problem has emerged recently. Because this source tends to preserve and strengthen any racial or sexual imbalance in your staffing, you must take positive steps to ensure that the rest of your recruitment programme redresses the balance.

People you know already (D-I-Y headhunting)

In any search for new people one can use a personal 'bush telegraph' to reach people who may be unemployed or potentially mobile among friends of friends, suppliers, customers and even neighbours. Asking a customer whom he regards as the best sales representative selling to him can be most informative, on several levels and flatters him as well.

People who have left

This is an extension of the above and a particularly fruitful source because their work performance is known. At any one time only a few will be relevant and only a few will want to come back but they too will be flattered to be asked and the reasons which encouraged their departure may no longer apply, or the grass may not have been greener on the other side. They may recommend others if they are not interested and the question is asked.

People who applied last time

Another free source. Given careful records of candidates applying for previous vacancies, they too may be flattered and receptive when approached again. If the volume is too great to consider keeping all the letters, forms and CVs a qualitative filter is one answer although this may weed out the mediocre people who would be just right for a less demanding job next year. Alternatively one could feed brief data into store, either on edge-punched cards or in computer memory if there is already a personnel record system which retrieves data selectively for personnel development purposes. Any such system must be made known to directors and senior managers who receive unsolicited applications from job hunters, so that they can record these people too.

Other volunteers

The unsolicited applications mentioned above come from volunteers, either as a result of continuing PR effort if you want to make this a source of staff or labour or just because you exist and the unemployed think you are a worthwhile potential employer. It is important to take them seriously. Most may be worthless, but the few which are not can save you hundreds, perhaps thousands, of pounds in recruitment costs if properly filed and retrieved. Consultants do so, because it pays dividends. They have no monopoly on this system.

Milk round/schools contacts

These sources are better for prior contact with careers staff, whether seeking a few key management trainees or a regular supply of clerical staff and skilled or unskilled labour. The bonus one can generate from employment agencies, by treating them properly and involving them in your corporate thinking, can also be generated from careers staff who are often fairly naïve about what goes on in industry and commerce, locally or nationally. However, they are likely to be intelligent and caring and therefore responsive to constructive input from the minority of employers who take them seriously. Two further ideas come to mind:

(a) Unless the volume requirement is massive, avoid the milkround and concentrate on attracting volunteers by good PR and limited advertising of specific needs.
(b) If turnover of graduate trainees has been higher than you would wish, ignore new graduates and try a specialized low-cost advertising programme unashamedly aimed at those, two to five years out of university, who have realized they are in the wrong place. They will be more mature, more flexible and more stable.

Mix and match

We have reviewed a dozen possible sources, approved none in isolation and offered advice on when to use them. Any and all recruitment techniques may be relevant. Few are perfect on their own. Employers need to choose a mix which suits the urgency and uniqueness of each search. They can also choose very cheap sources if they have patience or very quick ones if money is no object. The nice thing about the dozen is that half are virtually free, three only cost money when you achieve success and only the other three cost significant amounts up front before results are seen. This could be cost-effective.

5

Advertising: media planning

Before you decide to advertise you should have considered the various alternatives discussed in chapter 4. Advertising can be complementary to these, or replace them. Most people are more likely to find difficulty in advertising effectively than to use any of the other alternatives effectively. It is therefore particularly important to adopt a disciplined approach which includes a consideration of the need for advertising, its objectives, the choice of media and the assessment of media and other sources.

Advertising is not the perfect way of recruiting people. It is necessary. It is effective. If it did not exist someone would certainly have invented it. Unfortunately, it costs money. Badly used it can be very ineffective. It sometimes creates a massive administrative burden. If it fails you are back to square one with weeks (or months) lost. It follows that your consideration of other sources should be serious and that you should review the relevance of those sources to the vacancy with particular care. It also follows that you must define your objective thoroughly. For example, if you are looking for one senior executive of particularly high quality it may be acceptable to choose from a very slim response (by headhunt or other means) and a one or two person shortlist. Hundreds of applicants in such a case would almost certainly be irrelevant.

If, on the other hand, you want dozens of new junior employees, quantity is essential. Headhunting is unlikely to be appropriate. Advertising is a very likely source. These two extremes are easy. The shades of grey in between cause most of the difficulty. One workable rule is to select a source, or combination of sources, which should give the best sample of relevant candidates with the minimum burden of irrelevant ones.

Cost should also be a factor. We could therefore define our objective as the successful appointment of the right people within a reasonable time at a reasonable cost (not minimum cost). Free recruitment would be ideal and, of course, the most cost-effective form can be of volunteers, but they are not predictable. The next choice must be cheap, effective advertising. Less desirable but still acceptable is costly but effective advertising. Undesirable is ineffective advertising, whether cheap or costly, because time is lost. If the jobs are worth filling you are losing money while they are not filled and the losses probably exceed the cost of any normal advertising budget.

Having defined the preliminary target, we need to recognize the likely secondary ones, if only so that we can help our colleagues not to be seduced or confused by them. These secondaries often include:

(a)   house advertising
(b)   volunteers, for next time
(c)   stimulating internal applicants
(d)   industrial espionage (gathering confidential data from competitors' employees who apply).

Some of these can be achieved without prejudicing the primary objective, but they should not be allowed to interfere unless, as with (c) above, they are considered essential to the planned recruitment effort.

The next essential, as implied earlier, is that you clear your mind about media. If you read, you must have preferences as a reader. If you are also trying to hire a replica of yourself when young (even good job analysis does not always exclude this) it is tempting to assume that all candidates share your preferences as a reader. The exercise of a little common sense should demonstrate that they may not. Even if they did, any recruitment advertising agency has figures to demonstrate that the media which people read often bear no resemblance to the ones they look at for jobs. You therefore need to take advice (from an agency, selection consultants, personnel colleagues or your own records) about response levels, both quantitative and qualitative.

Response

Concentrate on response; it is essential to the achievement of your objective. Most unsuccessful advertisements fail by avoidable errors. The response volume (or lack of it) is where an error is least acceptable. If we consider the basic stages of a recruitment programme, this may be clearer. The following are the likely sources of loss at each stage:

Error	Loss
Wrong choice of media	Over half the relevant audience
Unattractive text	Most of the remainder
(including reply instructions)	Most of the residue
Unsympathetic processing	All the rest
Poor interviewing techniques	

These are covered in more detail below but we emphasize that if the choice of media is wrong there is very little to work on in the later stages.

What do we understand by 'media'? Most amateurs assume it covers newspapers and specialist journals. Most of us have to be reminded that it also includes commercial radio and television. For our purposes we should also consider posters. Sandwich boards and sky-writing are probably a little too extreme, but do not rule them out entirely. The sort of lateral thinking which could take one as far as sky-writing or the Goodyear balloon could also help in the future to identify unlikely media for unexpected or unusual vacancies.

The same thought process could also lead from the little slotted boards so popular outside back street factories (proclaiming 'vacancies/no vacancies' above a wide range of jobs) to a more sophisticated form which transforms your front window or reception area into a medium in its own right. You could also think, in conjunction with your PR department, how to turn your recruitment programme into something newsworthy enough to justify editorial coverage. Apart from the fact that this can strengthen your impact in some of the media mentioned above, it can also get you into two other media which do not carry advertising, ie BBC radio and regional BBC TV.

However, most of these are less relevant for run of the mill recruitment. Here we need to consider the traditional media and get a rough idea of their relevance as follows:

Media	Blue collar	White collar	Management
Posters	Yes	Sometimes	Seldom
Radio	Yes	Sometimes	No
Television	Yes	Seldom	No
Local weeklies	Yes	Yes	Seldom
Local dailies	Yes	Yes	Sometimes
Evening papers	Yes	Sometimes	Seldom
National dailies	Some	Yes	Yes
National Sundays	Seldom	Yes	Yes
Specialist journals	Sometimes	Yes	Yes

Within each category there are dramatic differences in effectiveness. Both readership and response levels can vary surprisingly between media which look very much alike. Historic response levels remain the best guide but, if you cannot get them, the best test is to see if recent issues of the medium under consideration carry a substantial volume of recruitment advertising. It must be recruitment advertising. Product and service advertisements are meaningless in this context.

Recruitment advertising volumes should be mistrusted in relatively new media. For the first few months it invariably means that classified advertising staff are rushing madly round, selling space at almost any price (even free, for example) to anyone they can find. During this period two rules apply:

(a)   only a mug pays full price
(b)   only a mug expects a significant response.

The effective media in each category are surprisingly few. The following list applies primarily to recruitment which goes beyond narrow regional boundaries, in the management and senior white collar categories (patterns for blue collar and junior white collar are different but equally diverse).

Media	Total number in UK	Cost effective
Local weeklies	Thousands	Several dozen
Local dailies/Sundays	About 100	A dozen?
Evening papers	Dozens	Most
National dailies	About a dozen	Four?
National Sundays	About seven	Three?
Specialist journals	Thousands	Hundreds

At first sight this suggests a narrow choice, but it should not be interpreted to mean that you can reject any category out of hand. You have three choices, all of them valid:

(a)   Use the media which have been proved effective already.
(b)   If none of the above are relevant, take action to make ineffective ones effective for your own advertisement.
(c)   Take a calculated risk and devise a media plan which complements safe but expensive media with a handful of cheap but apparently ineffective media which have particular regional or technical relevance. As above, take such action as necessary to increase impact.

All this assumes that you are doing your own media plan. It remains true if a recruitment advertising agency is advising you, although such agencies make much of their money from percentage commissions on space bought. However hard they try to remain impartial, there must be a temptation to include expensive national media even when their effectiveness is not fully proven in the immediate context. It is therefore important that you collate or create response data within your own organization. This can be fairly simple but you do need to know the following, in order to assess the response objectively.

(a) Specify your target audience.
(b) Quantify its UK population (or regional if you are recruiting people who will not relocate).
(c) Attempt to quantify the net readership of the media you are considering within your target audience. This is to some extent speculative but if you do not try the exercise at all you are totally in the dark. This data is helpful in assessing media for any vacancy, even before you have built up a valid set of response levels. It can save launching a totally inadequate advertising programme or one with so much overkill that you are buried in the paperwork.
(d) Count total responses. Assess them both as an absolute figure and as a percentage of the likely target audience predicted under (c) above.
(e) Count worthwhile net responses (both absolute figure and percentage as above).
(f) Compare against cost and space used.

In principle this exercise should give you fairly clear guidance for next time. In practice other things may complicate your choice.

Timing

Timing is probably the most crucial. Popular media tend to have longer effective lead times, but there is no point in using less satisfactory media just to save a week. By the time you have evaluated the substandard response you may have lost a month. The alternative may be to negotiate with your preferred large recruitment advertising agency and get a piece of their block space booking for the preferred medium at an earlier date than your sole small space requirement would secure.

The recruitment advertising agency has more to offer at this point. When advertising you need to know the right day of the week and the wrong times of the year; most agencies have a very good feel for this. There is also no substitute for their advice if you have all the specific facts of each case, but here are a few pointers:

(a) most daily papers with regular recruitment advertising volume have designated particular days for particular types of job. Find out which day suits your vacancy and stick to it
(b) Saturdays are irrelevant
(c) advertising too close to a bank holiday can be disastrous, but the actual effect varies from season to season. Check with the agency
(d) there is a theory that you should not advertise during the summer holidays. This may be nonsense. Certainly the total number of readers must drop off, but the number of advertisements declines more on a percentage basis so, in a competitive market, your chances that any one good candidate may respond could actually improve.

Repeats

Should you try the same advertisement two weeks running, or twice in one month? Ten years ago this would have appeared unwise. It would have seemed open to misinterpretation, even an admission of defeat. However, personal experience born both of desperation and experimental enquiry has now convinced the author that a genuine, incremental response will be obtained, especially in those media where the volume of advertisements is sometimes too much like hard work for the reader or, at the other end of the scale, where you cannot guarantee the readership will be unchanged from week to week. Media with a high level of pass-on readership are particularly relevant. There is one caveat: full price should not be paid for the second run. If you have to and are convinced you should, then consider changing the copy. Setting costs are usually slim in relation to space costs and you do want a new impact.

Quality

Quality can also cause concern. There is no doubt that some media attract a 'better class of candidates'. 'Better' in this context usually means more relevant, ideally with less response from unsuitable candidates. Unfortunately in this less than ideal world the availability of quality does not automatically guarantee the exclusion of rubbish responses. Some media generate a heavy volume of both. One way you can turn this to

30

advantage with a medium known for a good combination of volume and quality is to be ruthless about your advertisement text, making the candidate specification tighter or the exclusions more blatant (this is covered in the next chapter). Alternatively, there are a few cases where there is a genuine choice of media at similar cost and the two extremes reach appreciably different markets, but produce the same sort of gross volume. It is probably less true today, but a few years ago you might have preferred the *Financial Times* to *Accountancy Age* for a very senior finance post and made precisely the opposite choice for a young qualified accountant. Similar examples exist in most other functions of management. If the qualitative differences can be identified between media then the response can be significantly more efficient.

Cost-effectiveness

Cost is a problem for some. In spite of the earlier advice that cheap failure is unacceptable, if there is enough time in hand (perhaps for a post that does not have to be filled until a specific date some months ahead) a phased advertising programme may be planned which starts with the minimum necessary media. Minimum need not imply cheapest. For a major programme which mixes nationals, specialist journals and local papers you might well decide that a minimum effective starter is one display advertisement in an expensive but worthwhile national paper rather than a cheaper but less effective insertion in a medium which was only included in the programme as an experiment. You should also bear in mind that the drastic diversity of response levels can make a semi-display advertisement in a good national more effective than a massive display advertisement in something smaller. The former may even be cheaper.

To summarize, once you have decided that advertising is necessary, you need to behave like a purchasing manager acquiring products for assembly lines. You need to commit the necessary resources to get the right responses from the right advertisement in the right place at the right time. The means by which you do this are not always known to your colleagues, but they will certainly know if the effort fails. Expensive success is better than cheap failure in most cases.

THE OBSERVER SUGGESTS YOU SAVE MONEY ON ADS AND SPEND IT ON PEOPLE.

Looking for new people always takes time. But with The Observer it takes a lot less money.

Not only is space over three times as expensive in the Sunday Times and Daily Telegraph.

But The Observer also reaches businessmen at a lower cost per thousand than any other national newspaper.

So here's a chance to spend less money looking for new people. And more looking after the ones you've got. **THE OBSERVER**

Source: BMRC 1984. Rates at 18.10.84
Contact our Recruitment Sales Team on 01-236 1231.

What do the brightest and most ambitious executives digest with their breakfast?

Daily Mail Classified.

6

Advertising: creating copy

This chapter covers some golden rules on creating advertising copy. There is no point in choosing the right space in the right medium on the right day and then demotivating all the best respondents by an unattractive or misleading advertisement, yet thousands of job ads achieve this in a way their authors would condemn if the organization's product advertising were to be involved. This is the area where money can be spent and wasted.

This chapter will cover advertising content, classic errors, conversion of responses and some notes of caution. You may not agree with all of it, but every deviation from the ideal will risk damage to the total response, qualitatively and quantitatively. Worse, the quantity may not drop off. It may increase to horrendous and unmanageable proportions where replies to unwanted candidates become very expensive. Your objective is to attract valid respondents in reasonable numbers. Sticking to the rules will ensure this. There will be pressures on you to deviate. If you are the prime mover in a recruitment exercise one of your main tasks will be to prevent the action or inaction of other people adversely effecting the timing and quality of the exercise. Delay costs time, profits and enthusiasm. We touched earlier on the problem that gaining a week by using the wrong medium can mean losing a month by getting the wrong response. The more usual problem is that losing a day can lose you a week. Losing a week can also lose you a month. Losing a month loses the best of the candidates. This has to be remembered at all stages and it is no less important than when writing advertising copy.

First ask 'should I write it?'. If you know nothing about writing copy a specialist in your recruitment advertising agency might do it better. You or your colleagues may do it equally well if you observe the rules and adapt the techniques of the specialists, but it does demand some degree of discipline. The easiest way to demonstrate this is to contrast good and bad practice. Specifying good practice alone sometimes permits the inclusion of good and bad in the same text.

Good practice, bad practice

The good advertisement will:

(a) attract the reader's attention
(b) make the right people read it thoroughly
(c) motivate replies from the right people
(d) make it easy to reply.

The content which is generally agreed to achieve these includes:

(a) a clear description of the ideal and minimum candidate
(b) the job title or a clearer equivalent
(c) the type and size of the organization
(d) where the job is located
(e) the job content, if this is not implicit in the job title (which should be drawn from the job description)
(f) the rewards and prospects, if any
(g) some unique feature which sets this text apart from the others around it, for example, even if there are no prospects, security may attract the right people
(h) warm, friendly, explicit, easy to follow reply instructions
(i) a reference which identifies job, medium and even the person advertising, to his or her colleagues (this requires very few spaces if properly thought out).

Bad practice, by contrast, includes any of the following:

(a) omitting or disguising key information, as 'too sensitive'
(b) using box numbers
(c) including material which is really 'house advertising'
(d) orientation towards the company rather than the candidate
(e) excessively conservative presentation
(f) poor typography
(g) cumbersome, unclear or insulting reply instructions
(h) illegality.

Obviosly nobody sets out to achieve these low standards. However errors are surprisingly easy to make, as you will note if you open any medium at its recruitment advertising pages. Avoiding them enhances the potential success of any advertisement. The following notes are not exhaustive but they are based on considerable research.

Essential content

The first mistake most people make when new to recruitment is to specify the ideal candidate and omit to specify the minimum requirements. If advertising a superb job and you are able to be particularly choosy, this may be acceptable to minimize unwanted response, but there are few superb jobs. Most of those jobs advertised are going to be in that broad middle ground from mediocre to above-average which need all the response they can get. It is no use advertising the ideal, who might be a 30 year old MBA with experience precisely relevant to the job and your industry, when job analysis has also convinced you that the job could be done tolerably well by anyone from 25 to 50 with a poor degree or none and hardly any experience of job or industry. This is even more true when the salary offered is marginal.

Next is the job title. There are two pitfalls here. The first is to quote a company jargon title which bears no relation to usage in the real world outside. The second is to quote a recognized title without explaining the shades of grey which colour it in this environment. One company's works director is another's production controller and yet another's general manager. If in doubt, describe the job.

37

Describing the employer may seem unnecessary. Everyone in Braintree knows what Lake & Elliot do, but even before reaching counties where people don't know of Braintree, you reach people who may think they make art paints rather than hydraulic jacks. You are too close to your company to know how well-known or ill-known it is. The author has met people who don't know what BL, ICFC, GEC, EMI and MFI stand for. How much less do they know about companies in the next 9,000 rather than the top 1,000. Even if you consider that your brand name is well-known, people may not know what the company name is. Do you really know the difference between old Dekko and fast growing Deeko? Is PBI really the group behind Baby Bio? Tell people who you are and what you are. Even Rolls Royce (1971) has to remind people that it does not only make motor cars.

If you do not wish to advertise the job location it may be for one of three reasons:

(a)   you're ashamed of the town
(b)   you don't want your employees to know
(c)   you're due to relocate shortly.

None of these reasons justifies the omission. If you are going to lose people later when they find the job is at Sullom Voe, lose them at once and concentrate on attracting people who like the idea of Shetland. If you don't want your present people to know about the job, don't worry. If you advertise so imprecisely you will never fill the job and they'll never know! Instead do your internal employee communications work properly now and permit clear disclosure in your advertisement. Relocation is another problem. You have two choices. The first is to defer recruitment until you can hire in the new location, subject to a few weeks or months secondment at the old. The second is to disclose your plans in the advertisement and reach the minority of people to whom such a relocation (paid for by you) is an advantage rather than a burden.

Rewards are always a source of concern. Very few employers are brave enough to declare the true salaries and benefits for key jobs. There are numerous stock reasons for non-disclosure or inadequate disclosure. Here are a few, with counter-arguments in italics:

Other managers will be jealous
   If they're worth it, pay them more. If they're not, perhaps they know it
We don't like people knowing other people's salaries
   There are few salary secrets in most companies

If we declare a top figure, we'll have to pay it
In the author's experience the majority of jobs are filled at less than the declared maximum starting salary
We'll tell them the salary after we've met them
If you don't tell them you'll never meet them. People who want £X,ooo often won't respond unless they see there is headroom over that figure
Our bonus or benefits package will tempt people in spite of the salary
Benefits keep people but they do not get full value when you are hiring them

Money is quite often the unique selling proposition (USP) which is another reason why you should be open about it. If your salary is not the USP, then find something else that is. If you cannot stand back and identify something special about the job which would tempt the preferred candidates to do it there is no point in advertising. You might as well go away and do your job analysis again until you come up with a job/candidate combination which is workable.

Your USP might be money, location, security, early responsibility, prospects, good technical experience, association with a successful product, union trouble, losses, or even the sheer scope and nastiness of other problems implicit in the job. You have to decide but you *should* identify something.

Encouraging response

Reply instructions should be warm, helpful and simple. They should also demonstrate a constructive attitude to the processing of replies. Incredible though it may seem, some very reputable personnel practitioners still regard the following process as acceptable:

(a) candidate writes for application form
(b) recruiter sends form
(c) candidate returns completed form
(d) recruiter sends invitation to interview
(e) candidate accepts or changes date
(f) recruiter, at the interview, volunteers verbal or written job description.

Even the most junior candidate is entitled to be offended by this process. The best candidates will give up or never even start, in favour of an easier, pleasanter route elsewhere. The ideal reply route is a telephone number and a name of somebody responsible, who can disclose and absorb information at once and help candidates to decide whether it is worthwhile pursuing the vacancy. The next best in the author's view, if the telephone method is not feasible, is:

(a) candidates briefly demonstrate their relevance on one sheet of paper
(b) recruiter sends to relevant people a job description and application form and invites them to telephone to arrange an interview
(c) candidates interested bring the completed form or a good C V to the interview.

Other useful aids to communication in the advertisement are:

(a) inclusion of recruiter's name and title in the advertisement
(b) inclusion of recruiter's telephone number
(c) making it clear that candidates will get information (job description, company booklets, etc) in response to their first approach
(d) making it clear that they do not necessarily have to complete a massive application form before they find out more about the job and company.

Box numbers are virtually useless. Almost any alternative is preferable. If you must have anonymity, use an intermediary such as a consultant or the confidential reply service of a recruitment advertising agency. There are means to change the wording of a box number advertisement so as to reduce the disadvantage but it can never be entirely eliminated.

Finally, although it seems trivial, a reference code which identifies the job and each medium in which you advertise is absolutely essential, for several reasons:

(a) it will avoid confusion with other advertisements you or your colleagues have placed in the same medium or similar ones at about the same time
(b) it permits precise assembly of response data
(c) it facilitates later filing and retrieval
(d) if you ask for it to be put on the envelopes it can ease your mail opening routines
(e) if you are in the employment agency world it helps you to keep your statutory records
(f) it is a useful test of people's willingness to read and abide by the reply instructions.

40

House advertising

It is tempting to use recruitment advertising as a means to advertise the company's image, products or services. To some professional sectors where service advertising is unethical it may be the only way to do so. This is not necessarily bad. It can even enhance the effect of the advertisement if properly done, but it should never be allowed to detract from or take precedence over the primary purpose, ie good recruitment.

A co-ordinated recruitment programme with good graphics and recurring company logo must have some cumulative effect. If the story which the series tells is one of expansion and good personnel development each advertisement helps to generate response to itself and its successors. Only when the immediate recruitment need is subordinated to the corporate story do you need to worry. There is however a related problem. Often writers are so proud of the company that they fail to catch the candidate's attention early enough (or at all) with some indication that he or she could actually be in the running for the job described. Traditional advertisements give some indication of the company and job first, with the candidate requirement tucked away at the foot, almost as an afterthought. To catch attention, why not start by identifying the fact that the reader is relevant? At a senior level people may know that they want to be a:

Managing Director
British Computers PLC

At lower levels they are more likely to identify with:

Recently Qualified Chartered Accountant

than a job title whose implications they will not have the knowledge to relate to themselves. This leads us naturally to the sort of conservative presentation, both in typography and other things, which wastes much of the money spent on national advertising. Never forget you are competing against hundreds of other recruiters in a market place. You can compete just on the size of advertisement, but space costs money. Alternatively, once you have reached the essential minimum size for good noting scores (Esso studies in the late 1960s indicated something around 4in across 2 columns, although a little more may be needed nowadays) you can be noticed by good layout, striking border, popular logo, and/or putting your USP in large clear type as a heading of your advertisement. Conservative presentation is often defended by an argument that anything more exciting would damage the company image. Few companies would damage their image by the suggestions above, short of a headline which is gratuitously offensive to a large number of people. Almost the only thing which comes in this category is accidental illegality. Illegality is remarkably easy when one is forbidden to discriminate on as many grounds as are current in the UK. Traditional writing habits may make you put the male pronoun rather than the female and there are several other ways in which you can inadvertently offend. For this reason and because you will be your own least effective proof reader it is advisable to get somebody else to check your text when you have written it. The text could then be checked at the same time for truth, excessively flowery language, euphemisms, jargon and sense.

Advertising agencies

A good recruitment advertising agency could help you on all of the above, but they are not necessarily perfect. It may be a useful part of your recruitment education to work with and through a good one for a while. One of two things would then happen. If they suit you, the working relationship and the quality of their advice and the results will justify a longer term collaboration. Alternatively, if you learn their techniques but feel you could do better you may evolve beyond using them. You will not know until you have tried. One of the things an agency will seldom tell you is how to make a useless medium effective. Most useless media also have fairly cheap advertising space. If the one you want to try does not, this method is invalid. If it does, go direct to the classified advertising manager and explain that you want to try an experiment, to maximize response levels on a key job. If it is patently not a key job, represent it as a sample of greater things to come. On this basis, book a large cheap space in an unusual place (front cover, opposite good editorial matter, on a colour page or even as an insert) where maximum impact will be achieved even to people who are not looking at the classified pages. This can work, sometimes.

Checklist: accentuate the positive and eliminate the negative

Do allocate resources generously once you have decided to advertise.

Do group the media appearances together in a tight time framework.

Do take professional advice if you are unsure.

Do mention salary, location, job title, company description etc.

Do aim for maximum disclosure in the text.

Be realistic about the job to avoid overselling and subsequent disappointment at the interview.

Do identify the USP or otherwise seize attention.

Do write warmly.

Do help candidates to recognize their relevance.

Do make it easy to respond.

Do put your address in the advertisement.

Do process the results swiftly and sympathetically.

43

HAY-MSL
Selection and
Advertising

...offers the services previously provided separately for over 25 years by MSL (Management Selection Limited) and ASL (MSL Advertising Services Limited). These services provide a comprehensive professional recruitment consultancy offering authoritative, flexible, creative and cost effective solutions to selection and recruitment advertising problems – whether in the UK or overseas. Our services cover:

- Recruitment Advertising
- Selection Consultancy
- Preliminary screening
- Information packs and telephone response
- Personnel documentation
- Recruitment literature
- Training
- Psychological testing and assessment
- Recruitment and selection support services

For more information contact Brian Woodrow or Ian Lloyd

HAY-MSL Selection and Advertising
52 Grosvenor Gardens, London SW1W 0AW. Tel: 01-730 0833.

We also have offices in

THE CITY (01-236 5354)	**LEEDS (0532 454757)**
BIRMINGHAM (021-643 6234)	**GLASGOW (041-248 7700)**
MANCHESTER (061-834 2425)	**EDINBURGH (031-225 3307)**
BRISTOL (0272 276617)	

A Division of HAY-MSL Management Consultants Group Ltd.

SELECTION & ADVERTISING

7

From response to meeting

The period between your first contact with the candidate and the first interview is crucial. Correct action can make all the difference between brisk success and tedious failure. It can also improve the motivation of the successful candidate. Delay offends unless explained, it also loses good candidates to other employers. The aim is to get a reasonable number of good candidates to interview with minimum effort, losing none that you would wish to meet, meeting none that you could have rejected on the basis of their preliminary disclosures.

Unfortunately, you cannot always be sure what the volumes are going to be. It is easy if you are using consultants who will present a formal shortlist of three to six people, but if you are advertising or using a combination of the sources listed in chapter 4 the volume may vary from a handful to hundreds per vacancy. The early analysis which has already been recommended should help you to plan for a glut or a dearth. If the latter is indicated your reply instructions should have been particularly warm and encouraging, including a telephone number so that someone can make preliminary decisions and suggest an interview to each acceptable candidate at very first contact. It gets more difficult if you expect hundreds. Nevertheless, if you aim to treat candidates as well as you would like to be treated, conventional reply instructions and processing methods leave much to be desired. If you can be better than other employers at this point, the quality and effectiveness of your recruitment can increase dramatically.

Before we consider ways to make your organization impeccable, the principles of candidate processing deserve to be spelled out.

(a) Offer enough data and generate enough from candidates to permit a short but very relevant interview list.

(b) Encourage them to pursue the vacancy until you can decide that there is a mismatch.

(c)   They do not owe you any favours. You, by looking for employees, owe them some consideration. Keep them warm. Explain delays. Communication failures will lose the best people first.

(d)   You owe them morally, if not legally, reimbursement of reasonable travel expenses at interviews. Declaring this in advance has two merits. It makes you look professional to candidates and it also enables you to specify what you mean by 'reasonable', thus avoiding later bickering over inland air fares, first class rail fares, unexpected hotel bills and so on.

(e)   They should not expect you to work nights and weekends, but some flexibility at lunchtime and at each end of the day for interviews is good practice, not least because the candidate who is most conscious of a responsibility to an existing employer is likely to be responsible and dedicated to a future employer.

(f)   If the interview is likely to be long, with or without tests, they should be warned in advance.

(g)   If the interview location presents special problems they should be warned. Information on how to find it possibly including map, description and mention of parking facilities is important. Is the postal address the same as the name of the local station? Will there be taxis? Are there several gates or several sites? Is the company name visible on the facade? Does the receptionist know the name of the interviewer?

(h)   Unnecessary stress and confusion should be avoided.

Do not neglect the mechanical processing which arises immediately after first approaches by candidates. If you are using the telephone to set up interviews, do confirm in writing and also consider whether parts of the procedure outlined below could be added to advantage.

Paperwork

Modern word processing equipment can make the routines of candidate processing much easier and apparently much more personal. Only two exchanges of information are necessary. Employers need to learn from the candidates whether they meet or exceed your criteria, to decide whether they are worth a meeting. Candidates need to know enough about the organization and the job to decide whether to come to that meeting. If the reply instructions in your advertisement are explicit enough, their first approach can satisfy the first need. Your letter to them can cover the second

46

and suggest interview timing. This system makes application forms obsolete or delays their use until you need full data before an offer, reference checking or induction. This is becoming accepted practice. Application forms are a source of irritation even when properly designed, for several reasons:

(a) They deter candidates whose standard of literacy is low, so acting as the wrong sort of filter in jobs where literacy is largely irrelevant.

(b) At the other end of the scale, senior candidates who have produced a decent CV, may feel that the use of an application form is bureaucratic, less informative than the CV and ungracious as between equals.

(c) In between, those with sound CVs may have similar reservations and, for those with a short track record, you can usually learn more from a good letter provoked by clear reply instructions than you can from a pedestrian completion of even the best form. If they know they will not have to complete a form, the incentive to write a good letter is increased.

There are two other ways one could minimize the use of the application form. One would be to have a national standard form, imaginatively designed, to take the place of the basic CV. The second, which the author uses, is to have an application form which only has to be completed on those items omitted from a candidate's CV. This is used where the letter-only or CV-only approach is not feasible.

Doing without application forms brings new problems. Under current legislation and codes of good practice your obligation to avoid discrimination actually requires you to ask for discriminatory information at an early stage in the recruitment process. Most letters and CVs will not volunteer enough. It might be possible, depending on the extent of your recruitment activity, to avoid full application forms and just have a brief checklist, perhaps even unique to the vacancy, which says 'For legal and practical reasons we need to have the following information on record. Please complete only those sections which are not covered in your existing CV and return it with your CV.' Where the process is genuinely one of selection, rather than volume recruitment, this could be a useful addition to the qualitative filter. The format can also match your data input if you have computerized personnel records.

All of this section has been about keeping respondents interested. Flexibility, speed, warmth and qualitative review are all involved. The alternative is to lose good applicants, resulting in possible failure, wasted expenditure, bad PR for your organization, lost interest which may damage your next recruitment drive and in some cases a positive bonus for your direct competitors who hire the people you have missed. Good practice must be worthwhile.

Agency introductions

This section has ignored so far the candidate who comes to you via agencies or consultants. Some of the above rules apply but the filtering process also obscures your view of the candidates and may obscure or enhance their early picture of you. It is important, particularly with graduate or managerial candidates, that the intermediary is authorized to make substantial written disclosures about your company. The alternative is going to be that they all write to your Company Secretary asking for copies of the last annual report and make you distinctly unpopular for your lack of foresight.

The candidate report

Many employers miss good candidates and waste time on bad ones because they misread candidate reports. One of the major differences between the many employment agencies and consultants in the recruitment market lies in the content and quality of the reports which they submit to client companies about candidates. This can be a major source of communication failure between client companies and candidates. Employers accustomed to the all embracing three page narrative style may neglect or reject candidates described more succinctly. Interviews may become inhibited, candidates may bore by repeating data already given, vital data may be missed. People may be missed. The same problem affects communications within the organization.

It may save someone's career if we consider the functions of a candidate report. The functions differ according to the context in which the reports are submitted. It is the failure of the originators and/or the employers to appreciate and react to these differences which needs correction.

There are three broad contexts in which a candidate report can be submitted:

(a) as part of a short formal shortlist for a known and well defined job
(b) as one of many speculative submissions for a known job, competing against other sources
(c) as a speculative submission, with no specific job in mind.

The function of the report in the first case is the simplest of all. The reader can take it for granted that the candidate is interested in the job and is broadly relevant. The report is required to give enough data to interview correctly and to identify the candidate's weaknesses and strengths in relation to the known specification. More than this is probably superfluous.

In the second case the report must at least give the minimum data above but also it needs to act as a marketing document for the candidate in order to allow the reader to decide whether to meet the candidate and also to avoid misunderstanding by the reader. This is not to say that faults should be omitted. A report which shows no candidate defects is inherently suspect. Ideally agencies and consultants would be studiously impartial. However, reports are written by fallible humans who may be over optimistic about 'their' candidates' merits.

The third case is the most difficult. The report must, as in the previous case, give enough data to enable the reader to decide whether to interview or not, but without any reference points (about job content) on which to rely. Presenting a balanced view of someone's career without knowing what may be happening in the client company is extremely difficult. It is particularly easy to miss some detail which will make all the difference between relevance and rejection. In consequence the speculative report probably takes two contrasting forms, the brief 'he is your sort of person, do interview' and the long 'mustn't miss anything' screed.

All this can be very confusing to the prospective employer, who does not necessarily appreciate the differences between the various types of report and the reasons for them. As a result, time is wasted seeing marginal candidates and good ones are missed. Both sides should try to ensure that they compensate for or eliminate the possible misunderstandings which can arise.

There is one extra piece of information which the client company is entitled to get, but seldom receives and hardly ever asks for. Quite simply, the employers should know what has been given to the candidate, said to him, done to him, promised to him, paid to him or asked of him before he reaches them. For example, a shortlist could usefully be accompanied by a note saying something like:

All candidates have seen, discussed and retained a copy of the agreed job specification, organization chart, the last annual report and your employee handbook.
We have amplified the specification with the additional confidential detail which you provided at our meeting and we have stressed the problems which you described.

We have not at this stage administered intelligence or aptitude tests or taken up formal references. However, we have warned all candidates that the final candidate will need to spend a day undergoing medical, psychological and other tests.

Where we have been able to take up references informally from past employers or colleagues these are shown in the individual reports. We have advised all candidates to make their own informal enquiries about your group, rather than relying on our presentation above.

All the candidates are aware that they have been shortlisted and, given due notice, there are no problems on interview timing unless specifically indicated in the final paragraph of the candidate report. We recommend that you contact them direct at their home addresses to arrange final meetings. We have paid travelling expenses to date to all candidates not shortlisted. To avoid duplication or omission we recommend that you cover costs for the rest, as and when you meet them.

All candidates are actively interested in the vacancy at Stoke, as Chief Widget Controller. Where they have significant reservations, these are indicated in the penultimate paragraph of the report. Those candidates whose current rewards are close to or in excess of the starting salary specified have been advised that we cannot commit you beyond that figure, but they remain interested.

In view of the security problems at Stoke, we can confirm that on initial enquiry, no candidates appear to have close family connections in or from Eastern Bloc territories.

When deciding jointly on the detailed approach to take, employers and their chosen consultants may know each other well enough to take most of this for granted. In the author's experience, they do take most of it for granted and should not. In other words, both employers and consultants blithely assume a particular pattern of action and disclosure, without much attempt to find out whether the other's assumptions coincide. For example, some consultants send out full job descriptions with their first written approach to candidates. Others never let the candidate see the agreed specification at any time. An employer trying to decide between a candidate processed by the former and one processed by the latter might assume that the second candidate was ill briefed because he didn't care, check or concentrate. Disclosure of method would eliminate this sort of misjudgement. Similar criteria as described above are also relevant in organizations where the personnel department prepares shortlists and candidate reports for other departments with vacancies.

Selecting the Right Candidate

Five days
Non-residential
Central London

Held in March, May, June, October and November each year

Aims

The course aims to give an understanding of, and practice in the basic techniques of selection. It covers the basic selection process including:

- writing job descriptions
- designing job advertisements
- interviewing
- employment law as it affects recruitment

Content

The programme is highly practical and participative with much of the time spent working in small groups. Individual tuition in interviewing is a feature of the course. A demonstration interview on videotape is also included in the programme.

Who should attend

Line or personnel staff who are, or shortly will be responsible for recruitment and selection and have had little or no previous training in interviewing skills.

For further details of this and other IPM short courses please telephone the Course and Conference Department on 01-946 9100 or write to us at IPM, IPM House, Camp Road, Wimbledon, London SW19 4UW.

'Innovators not Imitators'

8

Interviews and the alternatives

The interview is one of the most misunderstood, mishandled and dangerous parts of the recruitment process. Even between a competent interviewer and a well-balanced candidate there is a degree of communication failure, subjective assessment, personality clash and unpreparedness which undermines the good intentions of both sides.

If we start from the principle that all interviews are defective, we have a slightly better chance of success. Some of the defects can be cured during the meeting, by the participants. Others are incurable and have to be eliminated before or after the meeting.

The aims

The primary aim is to see if the candidate is interested in the job and competent to do it. Where the process is one of selection rather than recruitment you also need to compare the candidates against each other.

There is no point in assessing someone who is not interested in the job and no point in briefing people who do not conform to your minimum criteria. This is why we have stressed the importance of obtaining basic information on both sides before the meeting. If we give the candidates credit for being reasonable people, most of them can decide as well as, or better than, a potential employer, whether they can do a particular job. Similarly, although they may put the best construction on their records when writing to you beforehand, few of them actually lie. It follows that the exchange of data before the interview can either improve communication at the meeting or eliminate the need for abortive ones. This is also a good reason for telling them about the job and the company first and gathering information from them as the second half of the interview.

An awareness of the defects of the interview can also make one more aware of the need to use other assessment techniques. The areas which

53

should be covered at an interview are derived from the formal candidate specification which accompanied the job description and are along the lines of Alec Rodger's *Seven Point Plan* which is worth further study but the core includes:

Physical (health, appearance, bearing and speech)
These can be covered at interview. A later medical examination is recommended if the health factor is important (or suspect).

Attainments (education, training, experience, qualifications)
Some idea can be obtained about these, but documentary checks are advised on the major points. Where the experience is skill-centred, set up skills tests. Add a technical interviewer to the meeting if you want a depth assessment on complex experience.

General intelligence
A very rough idea can emerge from an interview, but formal tests or past academic achievements are better guides.

Special aptitudes (manual dexterity, verbal skills, numeracy, mechanical)
A subjective impression of verbal fluency can be obtained but a test is usually required for the rest.

Interests (working with people, outdoor, intellectual, practical, creative, active, social, artistic).
Here the interview can work. Most of these will emerge in discussion and none is likely to be wholly suppressed. The only risk is the spurious emphasis on something too readily identifiable with the job content.

Disposition (dependability, independence, leadership, tolerance, acceptability, powers of persuasion and communication)
Some of this can be explored subjectively at the interview but this is the area where psychological tests may be used by those organizations experienced in the use of them.

Circumstances (mostly ability to meet special job needs)
Probably susceptible to the question and answer approach, but it is unwise to take a candidate's view. Ask 'How will the family feel about that?' or 'husband', 'fiancée', etc.

The problems of getting objective measures for some of these are the reasons why there are grave reservations about over defining the basic candidate requirements in the original specification.

Golden rules

You will shortly come to a distillation of things to do and things to avoid
and listed below are a few formal rules about the conduct of the interview
which can make a substantial difference to its efficiency and results.

1. The first is simple. Tell them what you aim to get out of the meeting
    and how it may differ from their conception of an interview. Run the
    meeting accordingly. Tell them what will happen next.
2. Have an information pack for them, to complement earlier
    disclosures.
3. Run the meeting. You should be sympathetic but you are in charge
    and unless you are assertive you will waste your time and theirs.
4. Unless you are a trained psychologist and know what you want to do
    with the results, avoid deliberate stress. Whoever you are, avoid
    accidental stress (from environment, interruptions, body language or
    time).
5. Decide in advance, when reviewing their papers against the
    candidate specification, what omissions you need to probe. Work on
    an exception basis and tell them you are doing so, so that they can co-
    operate rather than trying to give you a biography.
6. Read a good book about body language and make sure that your
    posture and gestures reinforce the image you want to create rather
    than eroding it.
7. Do not be afraid to tell them if you perceive a gulf between their
    technical experience and the demands of the job. This technique has
    three great merits:

    (a) if you are wrong, they have a chance to correct matters
    (b) if you are right, but they want to debate whether the job really
        needs that experience, you will learn more about them and
        perhaps about the way such a job is done elsewhere. They may
        even convince you
    (c) if you are right, at least they know why they may fall off the end of
        the shortlist and they will not worry about their interview
        performance or about their personalities.

8. Remember you are selling not just the job but the company and its
    products or services. Every candidate properly treated is a potential
    customer or future employee if not required this time.
9. Tell them the volume and nature of the competition for the job. It

looks more professional. It can help preserve their self-esteem. It can help preserve their impression of you and the company as communicative and thoughtful.

10 Listen to everything. Every word and intonation is significant. In particular, their questions are probably a better indicator than their answers to your questions. Do not talk too much yourself.

Alternatives

At this point, you could be forgiven for wondering if it is all worthwhile. The author has spent a considerable amount of time in recent years working toward less interviewing as an achievable target and zero interviewing as the ultimate objective. Better pre-selection based on paperwork *in both directions* is the first step. People are seldom better than their track record suggests. Sometimes worse, very seldom better. More skills testing is also relevant for the majority of jobs, not excluding some senior ones. Somewhere someone is already putting together simple software packages which may eliminate all or part of the interview process for anyone who can use a keyboard or, with touch-screen technology, for anyone who can read. This could easily encompass basic literacy and numeracy tests as well. Zero interviewing is already possible. If you merely want fit people who want the job, a medical examination and paperwork (including a reference) could suffice.

Referees help cut down on interviewing. Wherever possible furnish the referees with a copy of the job specification in advance by post and then telephone to ask for constructive comments, in context. Even the most sympathetic and biased referees can give worthwhile input if their professional judgement is put on the line this way. It does not always work if you do it in writing. We all know how easy it is to write a glowing testimonial to someone's good points without mentioning the bad ones, if we are keen to see the back of them. This is immoral but not necessarily illegal.

There are other alternatives. The McGraw-Hill book, *Judging people*, by D Mackenzie Davey and Marjorie Harris provides a very useful rundown on everything from astrology, through graphology, phrenology, palmistry and assessment centres to psychological and other tests. From their texts and the author's experience palmistry, phrenology and astrology are excluded from serious consideration, although some employers claim to have had massive success, for example recruiting Scorpios into the sales function. Graphology has limited applications. For a brief and usually

56

reliable snapshot of someone you have not met one might consider it, but as an absolute guide or a serious competitor to formal tests one could not. Assessment centres are well regarded and if you have time, money and support for the concept they must be a serious contender for selection work on key jobs (not necessarily senior, but important).

Finally, we come to formal tests. These do not include the Rorschach inkblots or the Luscher colour 'test', both of which seem to have faded in recent years. You may be surprised to learn that there are more than 5,000 psychological tests currently available in the English language. They divide into five main groups, as follows:

personality
intellectual ability
special aptitudes
attainment in specific areas of knowledge
interests (and values).

There is a wealth of published material, in and beyond the IPM booklist, on the use and abuse of these tests. Relevant tests, properly validated and administered, translated by trained users, can be a great aid to the selection process and help make better use of people after you have hired them. This is a field where you must take professional advice, but the results can surpass the best a competent interviewer can do in many respects. Better still, a few tests are emerging which seem occupationally relevant, which must be useful both in selection and management development applications. With so many tests available it would be unfair to single out a few for specific mention. The best known tend to be the oldest and it is arguable that some of them are obsolescent. Their merits may lie in their familiarity and validation rather than unique quality.

Do

Tell them how this will differ from a normal interview.
Tell them who you are.
Explain why you are a substitute, if you are.
Encourage questions and listen to them.
Treat them as equals.
Use short explicit questions.
Use qualitative questions.
Ask them to sell themselves.

Ask them what they had to omit from the CV.
Use open-ended questions and react to the reply.
Be prepared.
Say 'for instance?' or 'for example?' if answers are too general.
Build your assessment from the track record.
Assume omissions need to be explored (much of the time they hide
    something).
Force them back to points of interest if they stray.
Pin salesmen to facts, when they veer to generalities.
Ask about excellence.
Ask what they'll be remembered for.
Ask what sort of reference they think they will get.
Then ask why.
Ask what was different, better, stopped or started because of them.
Look for good points.
Concentrate on the things you cannot test for.
Offer them a chance to take notes.

Do not

Dive into an interview without preamble.
Send in substitutes who are irrelevant, unbriefed, uninterested,
    inexperienced or too senior.
Guess answers to questions.
Prevaricate over answers to legitimate questions.
Patronize them.
Ask leading questions.
Duplicate factual matters evident from the CV or application form.
Be offended if they want to make a case for themselves.
Be shy (do ask if they are weak technically on any points in job spec).
Ask questions requiring simple yes/no answers.
Be late, sleepy, exhausted, drunk, distraught, unbriefed or foul-tempered.
Accept soft answers.
Make your judgements early.
Assume the worst without enquiry.
Interrupt frequently, unless they are running wild (senior and desperate
    types do).
Get bogged down in factual material with other candidates.
Feel obliged to review all past experience or their choice of deviations
    therefrom.

58

Assume CV tells all in this respect.

Take their choice of referees for granted (do ask for alternatives).

Take first reactions for granted (do probe, it is in their interests).

Stick to what they have written (you could ask how the job *differs* from other places).

Look only for weakness and flaws.

Assume panel interviews eliminate defects of interview process (they multiply them).

Ask their permission to take notes (the offer to them makes this implicit).

59

9

Assessment and decision

At junior levels you may have to make a hiring decision after every interview. At senior levels you may know you have to make a qualitative judgement between several people seen over a period of weeks. Both situations respond to the same discipline. Recall the original criteria. Review the candidate's performance against them, preferably using a proforma unique to the vacancy, with candidate specification repeated thereon. Make a qualitative decision very soon after the meeting in the range of: unacceptable/marginal/could do the job/would do it well/near-perfect. Record the reasons for this decision, not least to avoid allegations of discrimination of any kind later.

If you are hiring everyone who meets the minimum criteria, you can proceed at once to the next step: rejection letter or phone call or both/offer/test for skills, etc. If you want the best person for the job, the temptation when you have seen someone good is to defer a decision until the last candidate is seen. Instead, the *first* candidate you see who could do the job well (or better) constitutes a decision point. You should immediately review the paperwork on people you have yet to see and ask yourself whether any one of them is likely to be better. If the answer is a clear 'yes' you might have a reason for deferring judgement until the better prospect has been seen. However, unless the papers on the people to come look better, you should carefully consider the need for an early offer or a move to the next step in your pre-offer procedure. The 'bird in hand' theory applies. Every day which passes without action increases that candidate's chances of coming under offer elsewhere and does little to secure the later people. Moreover, waiting for perfection seldom works.

10

~~~~~~~~~~~~~~~~~~~~~~~

Implementation

In order to make the offer properly, some time at the interview should have been devoted to discussion of the candidate's needs, not only in base salary terms, but also in the context of your corporate package. This should ensure that any offer made will not be turned down in isolation because it is perceived as too low. You may be outbided or the candidate chosen may decide to stay where presently employed, but you reduce the risk of making unacceptable offers.

To keep yourselves in a position to bid, it is important that you have expressed interest in the preferred candidate(s) at or soon after the interview. Explain delays thereafter. Ask for 'first refusal' so that they don't accept another offer without telling you. It is very important that you ask. Few people will contact you when under offer from other sources because they may feel it looks too pushy. It would be ludicrous to lose someone good at this stage after all the effort which has gone into the exercise.

The offer can be effective contractually and be effective as a marketing document too. It should be started and ended warmly. However, don't expect to cover omissions or restrictive conditions in a formal contract later. Demotivation or withdrawal from the contract may result. For example, even if the new employee is going to be on the same grade as you are, it is dangerous to assume that the corporate rules give precisely the same fringe benefits to new personnel as they do to existing staff. Typically there are waiting periods before eligibility for full benefits or in some cases any benefits on things as diverse as holidays, pensions, insurances, bonuses and share options.

Do ask for a decision. Do specify a date by which you want a decision, or a chance to clear queries. Mention any qualifying conditions (references, medical, work-permits, etc).

When you have an acceptance, write graciously to the people you've been keeping on ice. Tell them it was close. Tell them you liked them. You may want them next time (or this time, if the front runner reneges).

Strength to Strength

At the turn of the last decade an organisation was formed with the objective of creating an environment to stimulate the creative and entrepreneurial instincts of a select group of individuals. Those individuals now number 27 and the organisation is on target for a 1985 turnover in excess of £5 millions.

Along the way, entrepreneurship became track record, ambition became tradition and profitability was translated to a standard of client service that perpetuated success and fuelled growth.

Today, Macmillan Davies has resources that encompass Executive Search, Recruitment Advertising, Corporate Communication, Employee Literature and a totally integrated service to the personnel professional.

All of which is good for us, but also good for you because our strength is your strength, and from the contact comes the solution.

Macmillan Davies is essentially a problem solving entity. Your problem is our opportunity. We call it Added Value, but basically we guarantee you the thought your needs require, and translate it into fast, decisive and calculated action. Our hunger for success is your insurance. We never duck the issue.

For a straight answer to any question, large or small, play to strength call Macmillan Davies. Your only initial investment is time. Time well spent.

Tim Davies, Macmillan Davies Personnel Consultants, Parliament Square, Hertford, Herts. SG14 1PU. (0992) 552552.

Macmillan Davies Personnel Consultants

I I

Induction and beyond

An induction checklist appears on page 66 as an aide memoire. The basic message of induction deserves to be stressed. Effective recruitment can be made or broken at this stage. Extend this argument and you are also reminded that keeping people is cheaper than hiring them. Consider having a 'retention budget' to avoid a horrendous 'recruitment budget'. If you have neither, where are you hiding the costs? The IPM publication, *Induction and the new employee*, by Alan Fowler (1983) covers the subject in more depth. Applying the lessons of induction beyond the induction process is a useful discipline and can be highly cost-effective, particularly because it returns to the original theme of avoiding recruitment, rather than trying to do it cheaply. For the contractual aspects of the hiring, which must be done promptly if not covered in the initial offer and acceptance, *see Contracts at work* by Erich Suter (IPM 1982).

Finally, a few points for senior staff need to be added:

(a) If you planned to fire or transfer the previous job holder, make sure the deed is done and blood mopped up before the new incumbent arrives.

(b) Let them know how they may procure people and materials, how to charge (or relieve) their cost centre and their limits of authority in these matters.

(c) Senior staff usually have to meet many people in the company. Ensure that they do meet them within a reasonable time, but not so hurriedly that they become saturated and cannot remember the names.

(d) Consider again whether the job description used for interviewing is adequate and up to date.

(e) Ensure that any promises, undertakings and offers of guidance or support made during the euphoria of interviewing and hiring are honoured (everything from orthopaedic chair to new secretary).

64

(f)   Do not lose touch once the individual is in harness. He may look
      confident but he still needs reassurance.

65

Induction checklist

Successful recruitment takes time and costs money. It is important not to waste this by neglecting the induction process. Inadequate induction demotivates people, increases staff and labour turnover, causes disputes, makes work for industrial tribunals, increases costs, creates litigation, damages corporate reputations and in extreme cases injures or kills people. Good induction pays for itself, at all levels. Incidentally, induction at senior levels is not excluded. It is often worse than at 'blue-collar' level.

These notes are not just for personnel staff. Everyone involved in recruiting and settling in a new employee should be aware of the principles. People are among your most valuable resources and deserve to be treated accordingly. When the company is presenting itself to its staff, this is a vital part of the process of building reputation and goodwill. This is not an area where you can congratulate yourself if you are doing 90 per cent right. Induction has to be 100 per cent correct or it has failed significantly.

Acceptance of offer

An acceptance is not the end of the recruitment process, but an acceleration. You now have to convert the candidates into successful employees. The first step is the post-acceptance letter, designed to tidy up loose ends and make them feel involved.

Review your standard example and ask:

(a) Is it warm and friendly?
(b) Does it say you look forward to their arrival?
(c) Does it say when, where and how they should start work?
(d) Are starting dates chosen to permit them to be welcomed, briefed, housed and used properly?
(e) Does it tell them how to recover relocation and other special costs, particularly if there are tax implications?
(f) Does it encourage them to confirm holiday dates, paricularly if you have earlier promised to honour them?
(g) Does it mention company plans, which you could not tell a non-employee, but will be known to existing employees (or evident from the press) before the date of joining?
(h) Does it invite contact before joining?
(i) Does it remind them about P45s?
(j) Does it confirm other things they were promised at interview (special equipment, organization changes, car order, secretary allocated, predecessor fired and off the premises etc)?
(k) Does it forecast salary review date(s)?
(l) Does it enclose organization charts or list names of key people, so they don't have to memorize them all on the first day?

Have you had a chat with everyone involved in the selection process to codify everything they have forecast or promised the candidate(s)? (Managers get euphoric when faced with a superb candidate. If they have promised the earth, someone needs to know when delivery is expected and on what conditions. Are they reminded to note this after interview?) Has the job specification changed since you described it to the candidate? If so, what are you going to do about it? Is anything else going to happen that insiders take for granted? Can you defuse adverse PR?

Before arrival
Have you told everyone who needs to know including the payroll function? Is a desk clean, empty, ready and equipped with telephone (or, on the floor, a set of safety clothing)? Is someone briefed as 'first day escort'? Is there time in key contacts' diaries for a brief meeting?

First day
Is someone briefed to act as guide and mentor? Does the brief include:

rules?	corporate objectives?
prohibitions?	personal objectives?
safety precautions?	location of lavatories?
people to meet?	location of refreshments?
how to get things?	where work comes from?
how to claim expenses?	where work goes to?
clocking/signing in?	hours of work?

Is enough of the above common to all employees to justify creating an audio-visual presentation? Have you confirmed the brief in writing, in a booklet or handout?

One week
Have you considered sparing time to talk about first impressions after a week? This is valuable for several reasons. It makes employees feel wanted. It permits the correction of false impressions and misunderstandings. It can provoke constructive comment before employees get used to your corporate peculiarities. Do you encourage this? For weekly-paid employees, have you confirmed that they understand, in practice, the reward system described in your contract?

One month
As the final note above, for salaried people. Check again that you have implemented everything promised before joining, or explained delays. Has someone, during the month, explained how your performance appraisal system works and the criteria by which he/she will be assessed?

End of 'probation priod' (formal or implied)
Do not let it pass unnoticed. Take the trouble to reassure, encourage and redirect employees at this stage, or they may assume before *and* after the deadline that their jobs are in jeopardy. Did you promise promotion, permanence, board appointment, more money, admission to extra benefits? If so, have you implemented? Have you discussed past performance constructively? Have you discussed future prospects?

12

Staff retention

Most managers are probably honest and self-critical; they are aware when they have made errors of judgement or fact *but* there is one key exception: a manager's reaction when a member of his or her staff resigns. You seldom find that anyone gets near to asking the question 'What did I do wrong?' or 'What did the organization do wrong?' Even when attempts are made to persuade the person who has resigned to stay, these are invariably on the basis of matching an offer, not undoing past harm.

Of course there will be times when people who have been well paid and well motivated leave for a genuine opportunity which could not have been provided within the existing structure. The game, and it is a difficult one, is to find out when one can only say 'congratulations', and when an individual or a company has been given a less than favourable performance appraisal *by the departing subordinate.*

Termination interviews are full of pitfalls. An executive who has resigned is looking forwards not backwards; he wants to leave in a rosy glow, he wants a good reference. He rarely tells the whole truth; if he does, it is likely to be to his best friends in the pub or to the personnel department, if he respects it, under an oath of secrecy. One way to get nearer the reality is to set up a series of meetings, with immediate manager, functional manager, senior manager and personnel manager. The aspects of the whole truth told to each individual might add up to something like the real picture. Perhaps the best way is to make the discussion as impersonal as possible and to ask what academic background, training, skills and personality an individual's replacement should have; one should also remember to ask if a replacement is necessary. One might also ask if the individual thinks he has a successor inside the company. The answer will probably be informed and objective.

Having made a mistake one should learn from it. Preventative steps are necessary too.

One of the odd things which usually emerges when one asks why people leave a company is that the reasons they join and stay are not necessarily the opposite of the reasons they leave. This paradox is best demonstrated with the uncontrollable reasons, like death, incapacity, motherhood, imprisonment and, for some members of a family, relocation. When one canvasses opinions, it seems likely that people join for adequate rewards, job interest, career development, prospects and perhaps security. However, the absence or diminution of any of these is not always enough to provoke departure. If we exclude the other reasons which leave the employee no real element or choice, like redundancy, dismissal, early retirement and injury, we are left with a broad category which can be summarized as the employer's failure to motivate the employee properly.

Obviously some turnover is inevitable. The long-term company servant is becoming rarer and to some extent new blood is healthy, but losses beyond a certain volume or losses of key people should force any employer to examine the causes, which will usually be found in the category of lack of motivation. It is perfectly possible to run companies with turnover levels which would be considered disastrous in other organizations or other sectors, but it is seldom the best way to operate. Even in those sectors where lemming-like losses are considered acceptable, all or part of the losses may be curable. These losses cost money, so even the most profit-conscious, 'people-unconscious' management can learn something by analysing the root causes of each loss and its cost and possible cure.

To recapitulate, most reasons for people leaving are affected by or controllable by the employer. It may be that in a particular case the employer will choose not to correct a problem, but it must be recognized that the option remains with the organization unless artificially inhibited by statute.

Before we look at the reasons for leaving in detail it may be helpful to look at the warning signs: the symptoms of the turnover disease. Poor operational performance, indifference, backbiting, gossip, absenteeism, clockwatching and trivial disputes may all be indicators. The classic error is to regard these as the problem, when they are normally just symptoms of a larger management problem. We are back in the 'omission' area and this is stressed again because most of the causes people volunteer as their primary or supplementary reasons for leaving are errors of omission rather than commission. Most of the common ones appear if one consults only a handful of people: failure to communicate, failure to motivate, failure to train, develop, create prospects, lead, reward adequately, permit participation or structure jobs correctly. Relatively few departures result from acts of management and those that do are frequently reaction against an act which reflects or accompanies one of the omissions listed.

It follows that staff turnover results not from actively bad management but from management too preoccupied to manage fully. We have all been victims and have all been guilty at some time. The problem is to avoid doing unto others what has been done unto you in the past, and it is less easy than it sounds.

Staff retention is a continual process. It can be likened to rehiring your existing staff on a continuing basis. For a start, do your job descriptions for your employees describe not only what they do but their objectives in doing it? You may know what you are planning for their future but do they? You may know why you ran the department in a particular way for particular ends but do they? Would they disagree and could they be right? Occasionally you can reverse a decision of resignation but as a matter of policy you should try to stop the rot beforehand. Even a successful cure after the act of resignation looks like (and is) evidence of bad management. It is also much harder to achieve. The promotion, recognition or rewards which will stop someone seeking and accepting a new job outside will be less effective in persuading him to withdraw that acceptance. Even if there is no new job, an emotional barrier has been created so, if you have a possible solution, use it before the individual summons up the energy to quit.

Incidentally, resignation may not be a once and for all thing, particularly if the person concerned is leaving for reasons other than career advancement, that person may return one day. Staff retention basically comes down to keeping people happy at work: what makes people happy at work has been the subject of perhaps more books, articles and papers than anything else. Fundamentally this seems to reduce itself to the immediate job satisfaction, the right money and the right prospects. An individual manager is unlikely to be able to affect individual salaries or promotion prospects to any great extent but the following random thoughts may be useful. Outside the current context of government legislation, it is probably better to give some sizeable and some modest increases rather than giving everyone the same: it is worth really getting to grips with your company's salary administration system, not so that you can cheat it but because it is almost certainly more flexible than you think. Do talk to your manpower planning manager (not just when you want to palm somebody off on another department) if only because most performance appraisals are 'public' but most potentiality reviews are not. Do talk to your staff about their planned future careers. Nothing is more galling than to have someone leave for a promotion move which is planned for him or her within their present company.

Immediate job satisfaction is equally difficult to write about without getting into the realms of advanced management theory. The following characteristics are probably common to all good managers (and these apply to what a secretary expects from his or her boss, and to what a board expects from its shareholders). The characteristics seem to come in paradoxical pairs: the ability to provide clear objectives, linked with the ability to give freedom of action; support and backing and letting people make their own mistakes, a lively and critical interest but lack of interference etc. Perhaps the key requirement is consistency: arbitrary judgements and illogicality are the hardest characteristics to work with; we can all work for a beast providing, to quote *Punch*, he is 'a fair beast'.

No real human being can dance this angelic tightrope for long. The crucial errors seem to fall into the major category of not keeping promises and minor sillinesses. It is important always to note what you have said to a subordinate about future plans; an individual has only one career and he or she will remember every word you say (and probably exaggerate it). You may have many subordinates and it may slip your mind that a modest increase has been given on the promise of a review in six months. Make a diary note now!

Which minor sillinesses will demotivate a group of people depends on the nature of the group. One particular unit turned from a happy band of brothers into a snarling mass of resentment in 24 hours following a notice from a new manger saying 'Don't walk on the grass'. A secretary once resigned after the chairman told her never to use the front lift again, because it was reserved for directors—a rule he had just invented.

The signs of unhappiness at work and demotivation are legion but once you have got to this stage it is almost impossible to get back again. One way of avoiding getting to this stage is to rewrite this chapter yourself. In particular write down what you think the characteristics of a good boss are and what in the past has demoralized, demotivated or irritated you. Emulate the first and avoid the second!

13

The cost of recruitment

The theme of this book has been cost-effective recruitment. Recruiting the right people with the minimum direct cost and effort is the ideal. Getting the right people in reasonable time at a higher cost is next best. Getting no one or the wrong people is not acceptable, because of the practical and economic burdens for the company. Failure to recruit must cost the company the benefits associated with the proper performance of the job. Recruiting the wrong people probably brings part of that burden, plus the later costs of severing or retraining. Neither is cheap.

Looking at the costs of normal recruitment first, even the free or lowcost sources involve a substantial amount of staff time, which will cost hundreds of pounds or, for a senior post demanding numerous interviews, will run into four figures. The costs get larger when one is considering national advertising of search/selection consultants and agencies. A staff job at £15,000 could involve direct costs as follows:

National paper, display, modest size	nearly £1,000
Most expensive national, still modest	nearly £2,000
Agency, at 10/15 per cent	£1,500/2,250
Selection consultants at 18/25 per cent	£2,700/3,750
Search at 30/35 per cent	£4,500/5,250

To each of these one must add candidate travel expenses, medical examinations, tests (psychological and other) postage, telephone and, as indicated before, staff time.

The cheapest volume recruitment is going to cost hundreds of pounds per head. Middle management could cost £1,000 to £5,000, senior management more. These are compelling arguments for making everyone involved in the recruitment process aware of the need for good practice at all stages.

Appendix
Special cases

Expatriates

There is very little to add to the standard IPM work, *The management of expatriates*, except to say that you should avoid having them if at all possible.

There are several good reasons for this. They cost more than 'local' employees. Their presence is sometimes resented or at best misinterpreted, which is not good for local morale. They or their families have great difficulty adjusting to local conditions and have to return early in a substantial minority of cases (30 per cent is the average most recently quoted and some companies suffer rates as high as 70 per cent). There are ways to avoid some of these problems. Hiring good local staff whenever possible must be first. Sending genuine volunteers, whose spouses are also volunteers, is another. Personality testing may also help. Induction and familiarization programmes do too. Hiring people who have been in the territory before and want to return also works at times. However, the message is clear. Changing companies is unsettling. So is a job change. So is a move to a strange country. Doing all three at once is fraught with problems. Reduce the elements of change to two or at best one and you improve the 'survival' rate. Incidentally, the culture shock and disorientation for the family can be almost as great within the UK as it is when going overseas. There are theories that it is most difficult when moving from hilly areas to flat and vice-versa and changes in climate will always prove a problem, but whatever the reasons, do not ignore the trauma of internal relocations.

Given the high failure rate, unconventional but expensive solutions which avoid expatriate appointments may be worth consideration. Similarly, the cost of early terminations is much greater than the wages or salary *in lieu* of notice. We must add the cost of the extra recruitment exercise, the job not done, the temps who may be needed, the damage done in the job in some cases and the unquantifiable damage to the morale of the other people around the job as further and very compelling arguments for getting it right first time, and not for low cost recruitment in all cases. On balance, getting it right is more important and worth a slight premium.

Minority groups

Your statutory and moral obligations to avoid discrimination have been touched on earlier. I would like to make a case not just for good practice, in avoiding discrimination, but for cost-effective best practice in applying positive discrimination.

There is no tactful way to write this. It is a question of fact that employers in this and other countries have discriminated against many minority groups in the past. There is evidence that they are continuing to do so. It is reasonable to deduce that the cases which become a matter of record are the tip of the iceberg. It follows from this that considerable talent has been under recognized in these groups for many years. A positive attempt to seek out this talent and reward it properly could give you, apart from a warm glow, additions to your employee strength who are better value than the average available from the majority groups. This is also cost-effective.

Positive discrimination can be achieved by choice of media, careful construction of advertising copy, firm directives to agencies and consultants and positive review of advertising response. This principle can also be applied to unlikely 'minority groups' like redundant managers and the unpopular age groups (50–65). There are many jobs where there is no substitute for experience. There are others where loyalty and stability are more important than the alleged virtues of a high-flyer. Good practice and cost-effectiveness go hand in hand more often than one might expect.

75

Section I

Advertising agencies dealing with recruitment advertising

Compiled by Jo Matheson of the Appointments Service,
The Institute of Personnel Management.

ADPLAN
Ludgate House, 107/111 Fleet Street, London EC4A 2AL
01 353 0807

ALEXANDER ADVERTISING LTD.
Alexander House, 19 High Street, Uxbridge, Middlesex
Uxbridge 51615

ASTRAL RECRUITMENT ASSOCIATES
Astral House, 17–19 Maddox Street, London W1R 0EY
01 629 4451

AURUM ADVERTISING LTD.
Edmund House, Wood Street, Altrincham,
Cheshire WA14 1ED
061 941 5231

Ludgate House,
107/111 Fleet Street,
London EC4A 2AL

Tel 01-353 0807/
01-583 1412 (24 hrs)
Telex 885206

AUSTIN KNIGHT ADVERTISING
Knightway House, 20 Soho Square, London W1A 1DS
01 437 9261
Birmingham
Tricorn House, Hagley Road, Edgbaston,
Birmingham B16 8TP
021 454 7351
Bristol
Brunswick House, Upper York Street, Bristol BS2 8QB
0272 422681
Chelmsford
Nelson House, 23–27 Moulsham Street,
Chelmsford CM2 0XG
0245 350250
Egham
66a High Street, Egham, Surrey TW20 9EY
Egham (Ldn 87) 33962
Manchester
Scottish Mutual House, 35 Peter Street,
Manchester M2 5GD
061 834 8723
Newcastle-Upon-Tyne
Erick House, Princess Square,
Newcastle-Upon-Tyne NE1 8ER
0632 614044
Sheffield
Pegasus House, Glossop Road, Broomhill,
Sheffield S10 2QD
0742 680251
Southampton
New Oxford House, 114/118 Above Bar, Southampton,
Hants. SO1 0DU
0703 38711
Welwyn
22 Prospect Place, Welwyn, Herts AL6 9EN
043871 7052
Glasgow
183 St. Vincent Street, Glasgow G2 5QD
041 248 6171

BARNABY & TARR COMPANY LTD
Didsbury Lodge Hall, 827 Wilmslow Road, Manchester
M20 8RU
061 434 4513

BARRETT ADVERTISING LTD
Sovereign House, 212 Shaftesbury Avenue, London WC1
01 240 7991

BARTLETT ADVERTISING LTD
13 John Street, London WC1N 2EB
01 405 8694

BASTABLE–DAILEY ADVERTISING & MARKETING INTERNATIONAL
18 Dering Street, Hanover Square, London W1R 9AF
01 408 1818

76

For the personal
approach to
professional, effective
recruitment services
contact John Bartlett

Bartlett
Advertising Limited

13 John Street, London, WC1N 2EB.
Telephone: 01-405 8694.

BATES TAVNER RESOURCES INTERNATIONAL LTD
63 Carter Lane, Ludgate Hill, London EC4V 5DY
01 236 3681

BENTON AND BOWLES LTD
197 Knightsbridge, London SW7
01 589 1444

BOWDEN DYBLE AND HAYES LTD
Oakland House, Talbot Road, Old Trafford, Manchester
M16 0AX
061 872 6100

BRUNNING ADVERTISING AND MARKETING LTD
100 Whitechapel Road, London E1 1JB
01 247 6525

JOHN BUCKMAN ASSOCIATES LTD
Manfield House, 376/379 Strand, London WC2R 0LR
01 836 8866

HOWARD BULL LTD
Garden House, 4a South Street, Reading RG1 4HB
0734 591891

BYGRAVES, BONE & ASSOCIATES LTD
7 Rathbone Place, London W1P 1DE
01 637 0216/7/8

BYRON ADVERTISING LTD
Byron House, Wallingford Road, Uxbridge, Middx.
Uxbridge 52131

CAMPBELL-JOHNSTON RECRUITMENT
ADVERTISING LTD
35 New Broad Street, London EC2M 1NH
01 588 3588 and 01 588 3576

CHARLES BARKER RECRUITMENT LTD
30 Farringdon Street, London EC4A 4EA
01 236 3011
Birmingham
Kennedy Tower, Snow Hill, Queensway,
Birmingham B4 6JB
021 236 2671

CHARLES BARKER CROSS COURTENAY LTD
Graeme House, Wilbraham Road, Manchester M21 1BX
061 881 7272

CHARLES BARKER SCOTLAND LTD
18 Rutland Square, Edinburgh EH1 2BH
031 229 7493
Glasgow
Clifton House, 1 Clifton Place, Glasgow G3 7YS
041 332 7571

COGENT ELLIOTT LTD
P.O. Box 23, 46 Drury Lane, Solihull,
West Midlands B91 3BJ
021 705 8201

COLBEAR ADVERTISING LTD
Loversall Hall, Loversall, Doncaster DN11 9DD
0302 855995

CONNEL MAY STEAVENSON LTD
William Blake House, Marshall Street, London W1V 2AJ
01 734 9041

COPLAN ADVERTISING LTD
21/22 Poland Street, London W1V 3DD
01 734 2711/6

COUNSELLOR
Red Lion House, High Street, High Wycombe, Bucks.
HP11 2BX
0494 34545

COUNTRYWIDE ADVERTISING AND MARKETING LTD
Countrywide House, West Bar, Banbury, Oxon OX16 9SH
0295 57371

CRAVENS ADVERTISING LTD
Newcastle upon Tyne
42 Leazes Park Road, Newcastle upon Tyne NE1 4PL
0632 326683
Leeds
27 Eastgate, Leeds LS2 7NA
0532 436401

CURZON-GRANTHAM ADVERTISING LTD
Calsec House, 40 Russell Street, Reading, Berks RG1 7XH
0734 590295

DAVIDSON, PEARCE LTD
67 Brompton Road, London SW3 1EF
01 589 4595

DEWE ROGERSON LTD
4 Broad Street Place, Blomfield Street, London EC2M 7HE
01 638 9571

DORLAND ADVERTISING LTD
121–141 Westbourne Terrace, London W2 6JR
01 262 5077

DOWNTON ADVERTISING LTD
103–109 Wardour Street, London W1V 3TD
01 439 7111

EASON ADVERTISING
66 Middle Abbey Street, Dublin 1, Eire
0001 730477

EVERETTS LTD
New London House, 172 Drury Lane, London WC2B 5PJ
01 404 4073

EXTEL ADVERTISING LTD
Hazlitt House, 4 Bouverie Street, London EC4Y 8AB
01 353 5272

FARMER ADVERTISING LTD
Hull
Norwich House, Savile Street, Hull HU1 3EG
0482 29001
Liverpool
Bank Building, 72 King Street, Wallasey, Wirral, Merseyside
L44 8AU
051 630 2574
London
Ferrari House, 258 Field End Road, Eastcote, Ruislip,
Middx. HA4 9UU
01 429 0121
Middlesbrough
9698 Borough Road, Middlesbrough, Cleveland
TS21 2HN
0642 244024

FOOTE, CONE AND BELDING LTD
82 Baker Street, London W1M 2AE
01 935 4426

FORUM ADVERTISING & MARKETING LTD
154–156 London Road, Leicester LE2 1NN
0533 553255

FOSTER TURNER & BENSON LTD
Chancery House, Chancery Lane, London WC2A 1QU
01 405 8733

GAYTON RECRUITMENT LTD
156 Upper New Walk, Leicester LE1 9EF
0533 555444

G. S. GERRARD LTD
Lichfield House, 66 Frith Street, London W1V 5TA
01 734 6747

MIKE GILL MEDIA LTD
3 Henrietta Street, Covent Garden, London WC2E 8PQ
01 836 8857

GILLETT & BEVAN LTD
5th Floor, Precinct Centre, Crawford House,
203 Oxford Road, Manchester M13 9GA
061 273 4707

GOLLEY, SLATER & PARTNERS LTD
9 and 11 The Hayes, Cardiff CF1 1NU
0222 388621

GRANT FORREST RECRUITMENT
Pegasus House, 375 West George Street,
Glasgow G2 4LW
041 226 3711

GREY ADVERTISING LTD
215–227 Great Portland Street, London W1N 5HD
01 636 3399

GRIGSMORE LTD
325 London Road, Ipswich IP2 0BE
0473 57575/9

G.S. ADVERTISING LTD
Floor B, Josephs Well, Hanover Walk,
Park Lane, Leeds LS3 1AB
0532 432043

HALL ADVERTISING LTD
Edinburgh
24 Drumsheugh Gardens, Edinburgh EH3 7UT
031 225 1211

HAMILL TOMS LTD
PO Box 34 Oriel House, Oriel Road,
Cheltenham GL50 1XS
0242 27072

HARRISON COWLEY ADVERTISING (NORTHERN)
LTD
Mersey House, 220 Stockport Road, Cheadle Heath,
Stockport, Cheshire SK3 0LZ
061 491 2992

HARRISON COWLEY ADVERTISING (MIDLANDS)
LTD
60–61 Lionel Street, Birmingham B3 1JF
021 236 7532

HARRISON COWLEY ADVERTISING LTD
32 Queen Square, Bristol BS1 4NQ
0272 292311

HARRISON COWLEY ADVERTISING (THAMES)
LTD
Glen Island House, Mill Lane, Taplow, Maidenhead, Berks.
SL6 0AG
0628 37222

HARRISON COWLEY ADVERTISING (SOUTHERN)
LTD
22–26 Commercial Road, Southampton SO1 0GE
0703 26361/6

HAY-MSL SELECTION AND ADVERTISING LIMITED
52 Grosvenor Gardens, London SW1W 0AW
01 730 0833
Birmingham
Union Chambers, 63 Temple Row, Birmingham
021 643 6234
Bristol
King William House, 13 Queen Square, Bristol
0272 276617
Manchester
474 Royal Exchange, Manchester
061 832 7203
Glasgow
14 St. Vincent Place, Glasgow G1 2EU
041 248 7700

MERVYN HUGHES ADVERTISING LTD
37 Golden Square, London W1R 4AL
01 734 1200

GEORGE HYNES & PARTNERS LTD
New Mercury House, 82 Farringdon Street, London EC4
01 353 4030

JAMES OF FLEET STREET (SERVICES) LTD
184 Fleet Street, London EC4Λ 2HD
01 242 0101

JACKSON'S ADVERTISING SERVICE LTD
3rd Floor, Blue Star House, Highgate Hill,
London N19 5PA
01 263 0973

JPW RECRUITMENT ADVERTISING
Ludgate House, 107–111 Fleet Street, London EC4 2AB
01 353 5843

JUNIPER WOOLF RECRUITMENT LTD
22 New Concordia Wharf, St Saviours Dock,
London, SE1 2BB
01 231 7275

KETCHUM RECRUITMENT LTD
52 Bedford Row, London WC1R 4LX
01 242 1001

KIDDS ADVERTISING LTD
Leeds
Charles House, Low Lane, Horsforth, Leeds LS18 5DE
0532 587123
Teesside
Keld House, Allensway, Thornaby, Stockton-on-Tees,
Cleveland TS17 9HA
0642 612461

KINGSWAY ADVERTISING
27–29 Macklin Street, London WC2B 5LZ
01 242 8471

LEE AND NIGHTINGALE LTD
Marketing House, 25 Stanley Street, Liverpool L1 6AZ
051 227 2222

LINTAS: LONDON
Lintas House, New Fetter Lane, London EC4P 4EU
01 583 8030

LOVELL AND RUPERT CURTIS LTD
30 Bouverie Street, London EC4
01 353 0871

LOCKYER, BRADSHAW & WILSON LTD
178 North Gower Street, London NW1 2NB
01 387 8943

LONSDALE ADVERTISING LTD
Hesketh House, 43–45 Portman Square, London W1J 0JH
01 486 5877

MACMILLAN DAVIES AND HOWARD
The Old Vaults, Parliament Square, Hertford SG14 1PU
0992 552552

MARKET IDENTIFICATION ADVERTISING LTD
West Wycombe, Bucks HP14 3AB
0494 36471/5

MAY, WINFIELD & ASSOCIATES LTD
151b Park Road, St. John's Wood, London NW8 7HT
01 586 1171

MOXON, DOLPHIN & KERBY LTD
178–202 Great Portland Street, London W1N 5TB
01 631 4411

MP ADVERTISING LTD
York House, Chertsey Street, Guildford, Surrey GU1 4ET
0483 577341

NICKLIN ADVERTISING LTD
Pillar House, 194–202 Old Kent Road, London SE1 5TQ
01 703 6399

NICKLIN ADVERTISING LTD
Cory House, Bracknell, Berks RG12 3LE
0344 51061

OELRICHS ADVERTISING LTD
53 Wostenholm Road, Sheffield S7 1LF
0742 53251/4

PA ADVERTISING LTD
Hyde Park House, 60a Knightsbridge, London SW1X 7LE
01 235 6060
Aberdeen
12 Queens Road, Aberdeen AB1 6YT
0224 645566
Birmingham
6 Highfield Road, Edgbaston,
Birmingham BI5 3DJ
021 454 5791
Glasgow
Fitzpatrick House, 14/18 Cadogan Street,
Glasgow G2 6QP
041 221 3954
Manchester
Norwich Union House, 73–79 King Street,
Manchester M2 2 JL
061 236 4531

PERRARD FOX AND PARTNERS LTD
5 Hillgate Street, London W8 7SP
01 727 3141

PERSONNEL ADVERTISING LTD
30 Farringdon Street, London EC4A 4EA
01 634 1000

PETER A. MENZIES (EDINBURGH) LTD
Menzies House, 17 Rutland Street, Edinburgh EH1 2AQ
031 228 6565

RECRUITMENT BY DESIGN
Design House, Hanover Square, Leeds LS3 1BQ
0532 438991/2

REDHEADS ADVERTISING LTD
23 Quayside, Newcastle upon Tyne NE1 3NX
0632 321272

REID WALKER LTD
Lector Court, 151 Farringdon Road, London EC1R 3ET
01 278 3311

REYNELL AND SON LTD
Reynell House, 2 Station Road, Epping, Essex CM16 4HA
78 76435

79

RILEY ADVERTISING (SOUTHERN) LTD
Old Court House, Old Court Place, Kensington,
London W8 4PD
01 937 8100

RILEY ADVERTISING (MIDLANDS & NORTH) LTD
Birmingham
Riley House, Castle Bromwich Hall, Birmingham B36 9DX
021 749 3550
Nottingham
11 Clarendon Street, Nottingham NG1 5HR
0602 411656
Manchester
Trafford House, Chester Road, Stretford, Manchester M32 0RS
061 872 8163
Liverpool
13th Floor, Concourse House, 58–64 Lime Street,
Liverpool L1 1LF
051 709 6162

RILEY/MCS RECRUITMENT LTD
Newcastle upon Tyne
9 St James Street, Newcastle upon Tyne NE1 4NF
0632 612611
Glasgow
Rex Stewart House, 102 Berkeley Street, Glasgow G3 7LR
041 204 1771/8 and 041 221 9232
Edinburgh
26 Great King Street, Edinburgh EH3 6QH
031 557 4944 and 031 556 7242
Perth
208 High Street, Perth PH1 5PA
0738 20441
Aberdeen
11 Rubislaw Terrace, Aberdeen AB1 1XE
0224 641300

ROBERT MARSHALL ADVERTISING LTD
44 Wellington Street, London WC2E 7DJ
01 836 0381

ROYDS PERSONNEL SERVICES LONDON LTD
Royds House, 5–9 Mandeville Place, London W1M 6AE
01 935 7733
Manchester
PO Box 28, Bonis Hall, Prestbury, Macclesfield, Cheshire
SK1O 5EF
0625 828274
Wales
Avon House, Stanwell Road, Penarth, South Glamorgan
CF6 2XZ
0222 704373

SEVERN ADVERTISING LTD
Mason Road, Kidderminster, Worcestershire
0562 752876

SAATCHI & SAATCHI GARLAND-COMPTON LTD
80 Charlotte Street, London W1A 1AQ
01 636 5060

SAMUEL & PEARCE LTD
4/6 George Street, London Borough of Richmond upon
Thames TW9 1JY
01 948 2204

SEVERN ADVERTISING LTD
Mason Road, Kidderminster DY11 6AL
0562 752876

SHIPWAY COMMUNICATIONS LTD
Western House, Smallbrook Queensway, Birmingham B5 4HD
021 643 7301

SMEDLEY McALPINE RECRUITMENT
67 Long Acre, London WC2E 9JG
01 379 3233

ST. JAMES'S CORPORATE COMMUNICATIONS LTD
St. James's House, 4–7 Red Lion Court,
London EC4A 3EB
01 583 2525

STOWE & BOWDEN LTD
109 Corporation Street, Manchester M4 4DR
061 832 5533

STREETS ADVERTISING LTD
Hulton House, 161/166 Fleet Street,
London EC4A 2DN
01 353 200

THE MARTIN TAIT AGENCY LTD
Buxton House, 1 Buxton Street, Newcastle upon Tyne
NE1 6NJ
0632 321926

TATTERSALL ADVERTISING LTD
East Parade, Harrogate, N. Yorks. HG1 5LL
0423 504676

TIBBENHAM ADVERTISING LTD
112–114 Thorpe Road, Norwich NR1 1RX
0603 29301–6

TMD ADVERTISING LTD
20–22 Wellington Street, London WC2 7DD
01 836 3862

TOON & HEATH LTD
1266 Warwick Road, Knowle, Solihull,
West Midlands B93 9LH
05445 79321

UNIVERSAL McCANN LTD
36 Howland Street, London W1A 1AT
01 580 6690

A, VERNO & SONS LTD
15/17 Huntsworth Mews, London NW1 6DD
01 402 4122

VILLAGE ADVERTISING LTD
44 Wellington Street, London WC2E 5J
01 836 0381

C.P. WAKEFIELD LTD
Wakefield House, 152–153 Fleet Street,
London EC4A 2DH
01 353 3521

WALTER JUDD LTD
1a Bow Lane, London EC4M 9EJ
01 236 4541

J. WALTER THOMPSON COMPANY LTD
40 Berkeley Square, London UX 6AD
01 629 9496

WHITES BULL HOLMES LTD
Alliance House, 63 St Martin's Lane,
London WC2N 4BH
01 836 4466

WVB ADVERTISING LTD
12 Head Gate, Colchester, Essex CO3 3BT
0206 44606

80

Section II

Employment agencies

This directory was compiled by the Institute of Employment Consultants. The Institute sets out to raise the standards of professionalism and expertise of individuals working in the private employment agency sector.

The directory covers a spread of employment agencies throughout the country. The vast majority are generalist agencies, although some specialist agencies are included. London based agencies have been excluded, details of which are available from 'yellow' pages telephone directories. A list of multi-branch employment agencies is given at the end of this directory.

Further details of private recruitment offices throughout the UK can be obtained from the Federation of Recruitment and Employment Services' Directory of Members. The Federation is the trade association for the private recruitment offices throughout the UK. Its membership is nationwide, handles every kind of employment category and is made up of both small and large agencies. The Directory of Members is available from:
The Federation of Recruitment Services,
10 Belgrave Square, London SW1X 8PH
Tel 01 235 6616/7/8
(formerly known as The Federation of Personnel Services).

AARON EMPLOYMENT AGENCY
33 Silverdale Road, Tunbridge Wells, Kent
0892 21521

ABALKHAIL CONSULTING ENGINEERS
Adelaid House, Dun Laoghaire, Eire
Dublin 806943

ABERDEEN APPOINTMENTS
461 Union Street, Aberdeen
0224 575531

ABINGDON STAFF BUREAU
121 Ock Street, Abingdon, Oxon
0235 22271

ACCOUNTANCY EXECUTIVE APPS
47A George Street, Edinburgh, Scotland
031 225 5151

ACE APPOINTMENTS
Pauls Row, High Wycombe, Bucks.
0494 451616

ACTEL AGENCY
Actel House, Brighton, Sussex
0273 726585

ADDAP PERSONNEL
3 Melville Street, Falkirk FK1 1HZ
0324 36101

ALLEGRO PERSONNEL
Pine Tye, Lewes Road, East Grinstead RH19 3TD
West Sussex
0342 24096

ANN GIRLING STAFF AGENCY
51 High Street, Studley, Warwickshire
052785 3531

APPOINTMENT AIDS LTD
1st Floor, 59 Harpur Street, Bedford MK40 2SK Beds.
0234 45567

ASR STAFF AGENCY
24 Catherine Street, Salisbury, Wilts.
Salisbury 29305

ASTON PERSONNEL
1 High Street, Maidenhead, Berks
0628 72017

BAILEYS EMPLOYMENT BUREAU
36A White Rock, Hastings, Sussex
0424 444555

BEL CHAPMAN ASSOCIATES
62 Middleton Avenue, Dinnington, Sheffield S3 17QQ
0909 563369

BERTRAM PERSONNEL GROUP
104 Briggate, Leeds, Yorkshire
0532 442201

BLUE ARROW PERSONNEL SERVICES LTD
Blue Arrow House, Camp Road, St. Albans, Herts AL1 5UA
St. Albans 66264

BRYANT PERSONNEL SERVICES LTD
406 Union Street, Aberdeen, Scotland AB1 1TQ
0223 646238

BUPA NURSING SERVICES
St. Andrews House, Portland Street, Manchester
061 236 0773

CLARKE MANAGEMENT APPOINTMENTS
Norfolk House, 57–61 London Road,
Southampton SO1 2AB
0703 38046

COMPASS APPOINTMENTS
208 High Street, Guildford, Surrey GU1 3UB
0483 37433

COUNTY BUREAU LTD
34A Foregate Street, Worcester, Worcs WR1 1EE
0905 26671

CREAM PERSONNEL
48 Piccadilly, Hanley, Stoke-on-Trent, Staffs
0782 262731

81

DAVENTRY STAFF AGENCY
1A New Street, Daventry, Northampton
Daventry 2925

DEAN RECRUITMENT LTD
71 Lays Avenue, Letchworth, Herts
Letchworth 76739

FIFE SECRETARIAL OFFICE SERVICES
North House, North Street, Glenrothes, Fife, Scotland
0592 752312

FOREST EMPLOYMENT
16 Kings Road, Reading, Berks.
Reading 587272

FRASER PERSONNEL SERVICES
13 High Street, Hitchin, Herts.
0462 52771

GARNET PERSONNEL
10 Queen Victoria Street, Reading, Berks.
0734 597676

GEMMELL BUSINESS SERVICES
22 Maes Y Frenni, Cuymych, Pembroke, Dyfed, Wales
0239 739

GREGORY MARTIN RECRUITMENT
66 Park Street, Camberley, Surrey GU15 3PT
Camberley 20407

HARRISONS GROUP OF COMPANIES
1st Floor, Emerson Chambers, Blackett Street,
Newcastle-upon-Tyne
0623 610851

HIGHLAND PERSONNEL LTD
19 Academy Street, Inverness, Scotland
0463 239739

HMR BUREAU
175A High Street, Poole, Dorset
02013 6511

HOGGETT BOWERS LTD
Telegraph House, 7–8 Chapel Street, Preston
0772 23441

HOWLETT COMPUTER SERVICES
19 Bridge Street, Leighton Buzzard, Beds. LU 7AH
0525 382555

HUMBEROCK PERS. SERVICES LTD
343 Union Street, Aberdeen, Scotland
06517 2940

JOHN PHILLIPS SELECTION
Norfolk House, Smallbrook, Queensway,
Birmingham B5 4LT
021 643 9648

KEY PERSONNEL
12A Market Place, Braintree, Essex CM7 6HG
0376 42846

LEWIS RECRUITMENT
55 High Street South, Dunstable, Beds.
0582 601391

LONSDALE TECHNICAL SERVICES
11 Newmarket Street, Leicester LE1 5SS
0533 559711

MAINWORK LTD
24 West Street, Portchester PO19 492
0705 383331

MANAGEMENT PERSONNEL
Show House, 2 Tunsgate, Guildford, Surrey
Guildford 65566

MARGARET BAKER BUREAU
2 Care Street, Bristol, Avon BS1 1XR
Bristol 277456

MICHAEL LARKIN & ASSOCIATES
81 Merion Square, Dublin 2, Eire
0001 763562

MICHAEL MATTHEWS PERSONNEL
154 Union Street, Aberdeen AB1 1A1, Scotland
0224 639 76

NEVILLE GEE EMPLOYMENT CONSULTANTS
1st Floor, Britannic Building, Hargraves St, Burnley, Lancs.
0282 38942

NOVIA SCOTIA SELECT SECRETARIES
45 Renfield Street, Glasgow G2, Scotland
Glasgow 226 3885

ORS RECRUITMENT LTD
37B Witton Street, Northwich, Cheshire
Northwich 3556

PACE PERSONNEL
7 Old Christchurch Road, The Square,
Bournemouth BH1 1DR
0202 28371

PLUM PERSONNEL LTD
17A Market Street, Nottingham
0602 418856

PMC MANAGEMENT
5 East Parade, Harrogate, Yorkshire
0423 69961

QUADRANT EMPLOYMENT BUREAU
Regency House, Pump Corner, Dorking, Surrey RH4 2E1
0306 881204

RIDGEWAY EMPLOYMENT AGENCY LTD
34 North Street, Leatherhead, Surrey KT22 7AT
0372 374096

SAMPSON STAFF LTD
15 Piccadilly, Manchester M1 12T
061 832 4184

SCAN TECNICAL
9 Church Street, Bishops Stortford, Herts.
0279 58362

SELECT EMPLOYMENT
Trafalgar House, 8–10 Nelson Street, Southend-on-Sea,
Essex SS1 1EF
Southend 76426

82

SHIRLEY STAFF AGENCY
321 Stratford Road, Shirley, Solihull, West Midlands
021 745 1166

SOS GROUP LTD
Arndale House, Market Street, Manchester
061 976 2379

STAFFINDERS LIMITED
4 County Place, Paisley, Scotland
041 887 4271

STILTON STAFF CENTRE
32 Long Causeway, Peterborough
0733 60531

TAV GROUP OF COMPANIES
51A Market Parade, Havant, Hants.
0705 471711

THINKWISE RECRUITMENT
183A Yorkshire Street, Rochdale, Lancs.
0706 53321

TRANS PROMOTIONS LTD
1A High Street, Hythe, Hants.
SO4 6AH
0703 843913

TRICORN STAFF SERVICES
42 The Tricorn, Market Way, Portsmouth, Hants.
P10 4AW
Portsmouth 730494

WICKLAND WESTCOTT & PARTNERS
Eagle Star House, 16A Alderley Road, Wilmslow, Cheshire
SK9 1QX
0625 532446

WILMINGTON EMPLOYMENT AGENCY
87A Fishgate, Preston
0772 58934

WORKWISE RECRUITMENT
20 The Parade, Watford, Herts.
0923 28258

Major multi-branch employment agencies:
Head offices

ACCOUNTANCY TASK FORCE LTD
6 Broad Street Place, Blomfield Street,
London EC2 7AN
01 628 7931/7934

ALFRED MARKS BUREAU LTD
Adia House, 84 Regent Street,
London W1R 5PA
01 437 7855

ATLAS STAFF BUREAU
64 Oxford Street, London W1
01 636 4000

BLUE ARROW STAFF SERVICE
Blue Arrow House, Camp Road,
St Albans, Herts
St Albans 61373

BRITISH NURSING ASSOCIATION
470 Oxford Street, London W1N 0HQ
01 629 9030

BROOK STREET BUREAU PLC
63 Oxford Street, London W1R 1RB
01 437 7711

CAREER CARE GROUP LTD (ACCOUNTANCY PERSONNEL)
62/65 Moorgate, London EC2R 6BH
01 628 8438/9015

DRAKE PERSONNEL
Chesham House, 136 Regent Street,
London W1R 5FA
01 437 6900

KELLY GIRL SERVICE LTD
87/91 New Bond Street, London W1
01 629 0511

RAND SERVICES (HOLDINGS) LTD
37/38 Margaret Street, London W1N 8PS
01 491 3774

RELIANCE SERVICE BUREAU LTD
Grosvenor Gardens House, Grosvenor Gardens,
London SW1W 0BS
01 834 9177

SOS BUREAU LTD
2nd Floor, 60 Charles Street, Leicester
0533 23881

Compiled by
**THE INSTITUTE OF EMPLOYMENT
CONSULTANTS LTD**
120 Baker Street, London W1M 1LD
01 486 6905

Section III

Selection and executive search consultants

The list below has been compiled by the editor of The Executive Grapevine, the UK's only comprehensive guide to executive recruitment consultancies.

Abbreviations shown under entries
ES   Executive Search
Sel   Advertised position followed by selection
Reg   Register

A & A CONSULTANTS (HOLDINGS) LIMITED
10 Little Portland Street, London W1N 5DF
01 631 4184
ES Sel

ASHBRITTLE CONSULTANTS LIMITED
Seabrook House, Wyllyotts Mano, Darkes Lae, Potters Bar,
Herts. EN6 2NQ
0707 42406
Sel Reg

AUSTIN KNIGHT SELECTION
20 Soho Square, London WID IDS
01 437 9261
Sel

**ATA SELECTION & MANAGEMENT SERVICES
LIMITED**
Portland House, 29 Basbow Lane, Bishop's Stortford,
Herts. CM23 2NA
0279 506464
Sel

BARNETT CONSULTING GROUP
Providence House, River Street, Windsor, Berks. SL4 1QT
07535 56723
ES Sel Reg

BERNDTSON INTERNATIONAL
6 Westminster Palace Gardens, Artillery Row, London
SW1P 1RL
01 222 5555
ES

BIS APPLIED SYSTEMS LIMITED
Executive Selection Division, York House, 199 Westminster
Bridge Road, London SE1 7UT
01 633 0866
ES Sel

BOS RECRUITMENT GROUP
23 Pack Horse Walk, Huddersfield,
West Yorkshire HD1 2RT
0484 42730
Sel Reg

BOYDEN INTERNATIONAL LIMITED
148 Buckingham Palace Road, London SW1W 9TR
01 730 5292
ES

BULL HOLMES (MANAGEMENT) LIMITED
45 Albemerle Street, London WIX 3FE
01 493 0742
Sel

CALDWELL PARTNERS INTERNATIONAL
29 Buckingham Gate, London SW1E 6LB
01 834 7966
ES

CAMBRIDGE RECRUITMENT CONSULTANTS
1a Rose Crescent, Cambridge CB2 3LL
0223 311316
Sel

CANNY BOWEN & ASSOCIATES LIMITED
14 Regent Street, London SW1Y 4PH
01 839 2561
ES

CAPP ASSOCIATES
96d Southend, Croydon
01 686 993
Sel Reg

CAREER PLAN
Chichester House, Chichester Rents, London WC2
01 242 5775
ES Sel Reg

CHARLES BARKER MANAGEMENT SELECTION INTERNATIONAL LIMITED
30 Farringdon Street, London EC4A 4EA
01 634 1000
ES Sel

CHRISTOPHER TILLY & ASSOCIATES LIMITED
20 Harcourt House, 19 Cavendish Square,
London W1M 9AB
01 491 3393
ES

CORPORATE CONSULTING GROUP
24 Buckingham Gate, London SW1
01 828 1123
ES

COURTENAY ASSOCIATES
11 Maddox Street, London W1R 9LE
01 499 1875
ES Sel

CRIPPS SEARS & ASSOCIATES LIMITED
Burne House, 88–89 High Holborn, London
WC1V 6LH
01 404 5701
ES Sel

DANIELS BATES PARTNERSHIP
Josephs Walk, Park Lane, Leeds LS3 1AB
0532 461671
Sel

DIRK DEGENHART & PARTNERS LIMITED
4 Priory Gardens, London W4 1TT
01 994 2157
ES Sel

DIRECTORSHIP APPOINTMENTS LIMITED
7 Cavendish Square, London W1M 9HA
01 637 2171
ES

DM MANAGEMENT CONSULTANTS LIMITED
33 Gresse Street, London W1P 1PN
01 631 0303
ES

EGON ZEHNDER INTERNATIONAL
87 Jermyn Street, London SW1Y 6JD
01 930 9311
ES

ELECTRONICS RECRUITMENT COMPANY
Temple House, 25–26 High Street, Lewes, East Sussex
BN7 2LU
07916 71271
Es Sel Reg

E M A MANAGEMENT PERSONNEL LIMITED
Halton House, 20/23 Holborn, London
EC1N 2JD
01 242 7773
ES Sel

EXECUTIVE APPOINTMENTS LIMITED
18 Grosvenor Street, London W1X 9FD
01 499 0513
ES

EXECUTIVE SEARCH LIMITED
8a Symons Street, Sloane Square, London SW3 2TJ
01 370 0137
ES

FINANCIAL MANAGEMENT SELECTION LIMITED
21 Cork Street, London W1X 1HB
01 439 6911
ES Sel Reg

GODDARD KAY ROGERS & ASSOCIATES LIMITED
Old London House, 32 St James's Square,
London SW1Y 4JR
01 930 5100
ES

GROSVENOR STEWART LIMITED
62 Pall Mall, London SW1
01 930 7966
ES Sel

HANDY ASSOCIATES INTERNATIONAL INC
148 Buckingham Palace Road, London SW1W 9TR
01 730 8176
ES

HEIDRICK & STRUGGLES INTERNATIONAL
25–28 Old Burlington Street, London W1X 2BD
01 734 9091
ES

HIGSON PING LIMITED
110 Jermyn Street, London SW1
01 930 4196
ES Sel

HOGGETT BOWERS PLC
Sutherland House, 5/6 Argyll Street, London W1E 6EZ
01 734 6852
ES Sel
also with offices in Birmingham, Cardiff, Glasgow, Leeds,
Manchester and Newcastle upon Tyne

HOTEL RESOURCES INTERNATIONAL
87 Jermyn Street, London SW1Y 6JD
01 839 4450
ES Sel

HUNTER PERSONNEL (UK) LIMITED
49 London Road, Sevenoaks, Kent TN13 1AR
0732 45307
Reg Sel

INBUCON MANAGEMENT CONSULTANTS LIMITED
197 Knightsbridge, London SW7 1RN
01 584 6171
ES Sel Reg

JOHN COURTIS & PARTNERS LIMITED
104 Marylebone Lane, London W1M 5FU
01 486 6849
ES Sel

A T KEARNEY LIMITED
134 Piccadilly, London W1V 9FJ
01 499 7181
ES

KIERNAN & COMPANY
23 St James's Square, London SW1A 1HE
01 839 7384
ES

KORN/FERRY INTERNATIONAL LIMITED
Norfolk House, 31 St James's Square,
London SW1Y 4JL
01 930 4334
ES

KYNASTON INTERNATIONAL
Astral House, 17/19 Maddox Street, London W1R 0ET
01 629 3727
ES Sel

LESLIE COULTHARD ASSOCIATES
St Alphage House, Fore Street, London EC2Y 5DA
01 588 2966
ES

LUNAN INTERNATIONAL LTD
172 London Road, Guildford GU1 1XR
0483 574382
ES Sel

MANAGEMENT APPOINTMENTS LIMITED
Finland House, 56 Haymarket, London SW1Y 4RN
01 930 6314
ES Sel

MARC ST JAMES & PARTNERS LTD
5th Floor, Finland House, 56 Haymarket,
London SWIY 4RS
01 839 3701

MARKETING APPOINTMENTS LIMITED
11 Garrick Street, Covent Garden, London WC2E 9AR
01 379 7879
ES Sel

MARLAR INTERNATIONAL LIMITED
14 Grosvenor Place, London SW1X 7HM
01 235 9614
ES

MD SELECTION SERVICES
Wira House, West Park Ring Road, Leeds LS16 6EB
0532 744644
ES Sel

MERTON ASSOCIATES (CONSULTANTS) LIMITED
Merton House, 70 Grafton Way, London W1P 5LN
01 388 2051
ES Sel

MSL GROUP INTERNATIONAL
52 Grosvenor Gardens, London SW1W 0AW
01 730 0833
ES Sel Reg

M & S MANAGEMENT SERVICES
The Glasgow International Business Centre,
50 Darnley Street, Glasgow G41 2TY
041 429 2144
ES Sel

NOEL ALEXANDER ASSOCIATES
70 Queen Victoria Street, London EC4N 4SJ
01 248 2256
Es Sel

NORTH BRITISH MANAGEMENT SERVICES LIMITED
King William House, Market Place, Hull HU1 1RB
0482 224181

OCC COMPUTER PERSONNEL (SOUTHERN) LIMITED
Craven House, 121 Kingsway, London WC2B 6PA
01 242 9356
ES Sel

ODGERS AND COMPANY LIMITED
One Old Bond Street, London W1X 3TD
01 499 8811
ES Reg

THE OFFICERS' ASSOCIATION
48 Pall Mall, London SW1Y 5JY
01 930 0125
Reg

PA MANAGEMENT CONSULTANTS LIMITED
Hyde Park House, 60a Knightsbridge, London SW1X 7LE
01 235 6060
ES Sel Reg

PLUMBLEY/ENDICOTT & ASSOCIATES LIMITED
Premier House, 150 Southampton Row,
London WC1B 5AL
01 278 3117
ES

PURCON CONSULTANTS LTD
40 Lower Kings Road, Berkhamsted, Herts HP4 2AA
04427 75931/2
SE Sel Reg

ROBERT PURVIS CONSULTANTS LIMITED
Prudential Buildings, 22 Broad Street, Hereford HR4 9DR
0432 269668
Sel

REP CONSULTANTS LIMITED
14 Barker Street, Nantwich, Cheshire CW5 5SY
0270 626828
ES Sel Reg

SABRE INTERNATIONAL SEARCH
Seymour House, 17 Shouldham Street, London W1
01 262 7293
ES

R F SCOTT
16 Lord Chancellor Walk, Kingston, Surrey
01 949 4594

SELLECK ASSOCIATES (UK) LIMITED
Prospect House, 17 North Hill, Colchester, Essex CO1 1DZ
0206 65252
ES Sel Reg

SLATER-PACKARD TRAINING
Sales & Marketing Techniques Ltd
1 Museum Street, Ipswich,
Suffolk IP1 1HQ
Reg

SPENCER STUART & ASSOCIATES LIMITED
Brook House, 113 Park Lane, London W1Y 4HJ
01 493 1238
ES

STAR EXECUTIVES LIMITED
184/188 Oxford Street, London W1N 8AJ
01 580 0843
ES Sel Reg

STEPHENS ASSOCIATES
44 Carter Lane, London EC4V 5BX
01 236 7307
ES Sel

STOKES THORPE AND ASSOCIATES LTD
1 Fairfield Avenue, Staines,
Middlesex 2WI8 4AB
0784 59048
Es Sel Reg

SURVEYOR'S APPOINTMENTS CONSULTANCY
12 Great George Street, London SW1P 3AD
01 222 7000

TALENT BROKERS LIMITED
20 Maddox Street, London W1R 9PG
01 499 4288
Sel

TALENTMARK LIMITED
5–11 Westbourne Grove, London W2 4AU
01 229 2266
Sel Reg

TASA INTERNATIONAL AG
17/18 Old Bond Street, London W1X 3DA
01 409 2260
ES

TRANS PROMOTIONS LIMITED
137/139 High Street, Guildford GU1 3AD
0483 502525
ES Sel Reg

TRANSPORT & DISTRIBUTION MANAGEMENT
SELECTION
221 Streatham High Road, London SW16 6JL
01 677 7474
ES Sel
also office in Birmingham

TYZACK & PARTNERS LIMITED
10 Hallam Street, London W1N 6DJ
01 580 2924
ES Sel

URQUHART PARK SETON LIMITED
44 Victoria Street, Aberdeen
0224 632656
ES Sel Reg

Compiled by
EXECUTIVE GRAPEVINE
79 Manor Way, Blackheath, London SE3 9XG
01 318 4462

Bibliography

CANNON J. *Cost Effective Personnel Decisions*. London, IPM, 1979
MACKENZIE DAVEY D. and HARRIS M. *Judging People*. Maidenhead, McGraw Hill, 1982
FLETCHER J. *The Interview at Work*. London, Duckworth, 1973
FOWLER A. *Getting Off to a Good Start*. London, IPM, 1983
LEWIS B. *The Management of Expatriates*. London, IPM, 1982
LEWIS D. *Essentials of Employment Law*. London, IPM, 1983
SUTER E. *Contracts at Work*. London, IPM, 1982
UNGERSON B. *How to Write a Job Description*. London, IPM, 1983
WHITING E. *How to Get Your Employment Costs Right*. London, Institute of Chartered Accountants, 1984